'Please Leave Us Alone'

(The true and terrifying story of an Irish family and their desperate fight against the 'Hat Man' and Supernatural Forces.)

By Malcolm Robinson

ISBN: 9798480972146

(c) Malcolm Robinson 2021

DISCLAIMER

The author gratefully acknowledges the permission granted to reproduce the copyright material in this book. Every effort has been made to trace copyright holders and to obtain their permission for the use of copyright material. The author apologises for any errors or omissions in the book and would be grateful if notified of any corrections that should be incorporated in future reprints or editions of this book.

This book is dedicated to all those going through 'Hat Man'
experiences.
(My thoughts are with you)

Book Cover by Jason Gleaves – UFONLY

jasonufonly@outlook.com

www.facebook.com/ufonly

www.youtube.com/ufonly

www.twitter.com/@jasonufonly

Please note.

Due to the protection of some of the witnesses in this book,

a pseudonym has been given.

Non Fiction / Body, Mind & Spirit / Parapsychology /
Unexplained Phenomena

Other books by Malcolm Robinson

UFO Case Files of Scotland (Volume 1)

UFO Case Files of Scotland (Volume 2)

Paranormal Case Files of Great Britain (Volume 1)

Paranormal Case Files of Great Britain (Volume 2)

Paranormal Case Files of Great Britain (Volume 3)

The Monsters of Loch Ness (The History and the Mystery)

The Dechmont Woods UFO Incident (An Ordinary Day, An

Extraordinary Event)

The Sauchie Poltergeist (And other Scottish Ghostly Tales)

(All by Publish Nation www.publishnation.co.uk)

CONTENTS

About the Author.   Page 1

Author's Foreword: Page 3

Chapter One: Amanda And I.   Page 5

Chapter Two: More Bizarre Occurrences.   Page 23

Chapter Three: Friends Confirm the Bizarre Occurrences. Page 87

Chapter Four: 'Hat Man' Experiences As Told By Others. Page 98

Chapter Five: The Author's Thoughts.   Page 172

References: Page 191

Further Reading: Page 192

U.K. Paranormal Societies: Page 196

To Contact The Author: Page 197

ABOUT THE AUTHOR

Malcolm been interested in the strange world of UFOs and the paranormal for as long as he can remember, and in 1979 he formed his own research society entitled, Strange Phenomena Investigations, (SPI). The aims of SPI are to collect, research, and publish, accounts relating to most aspects of strange phenomena, and to purposely endevour to try and come up with some answers to account for what at present eludes us. Articles by Malcolm, have appeared in many of the world's UFO and Paranormal magazines. Malcolm has assisted many of the U.K.'s National and Regional newspapers in connection with stories concerning ghosts, poltergeists and UFOs. He has also been interviewed by many of the U.K.'s major (and minor) radio stations regarding the unexplained. Malcolm has also travelled extensively throughout the U.K. on research projects, and has lectured to various clubs and societies throughout Scotland, England, Ireland, United States of America, The Netherlands, and France.

Malcolm's television work has seen him appearing on Scottish Television, BBC Reporting Scotland News. Scottish Television News (STV), American Television's 'Sightings' programme. He has also worked for Japanese Television, German Television, Mexican Television, Australian Television, and Italian Television. Malcolm has also appeared twice on the Michael Aspel show, 'Strange But True' and has appeared on Grampian Television, and completed documentaries for BBC Scotland, (Cracking Stories) and the BBC 2 programmes, 'Strange Days' and 'The Right To Differ'. Malcolm has also appeared on live television with both Lorraine Kelly and Eammon Holmes at the G.M.T.V. television studios in London. Malcolm has also appeared on the Disney Channel and LWTV's 'Ultimate Questions'. Plus the Chris Moyles Channel 5 show, and also UK Horizons 'Paranormal Files'. Malcolm has also appeared alongside Melinda Messenger and Richard Arnold (Loose Lips). And has also been featured on the SKY

Discovery Channel, and was also featured on the live breakfast television programme 'This Morning' hosted by Amanda Holden and Philip Schofield. Malcolm has also completed documentaries for the Paranormal and Unexplained channels on SKY Television and had also appeared on Channel 5's Conspiracy programme and the SKY History Channel. These are but some, of the many T.V. shows that Malcolm has participated in over the years. Malcolm was the very first Scottish UFO researcher to speak on UFOs in America (Laughlin Nevada USA in February 2009). He was also the first Scotsman to speak on UFOs in France (Strasbourg) and was also the first Scotsman to lecture on UFOs in Holland (Utrecht). Another interesting fact is, that Malcolm is one of the few people on this planet to have gone down into the depths of Loch Ness in a submarine. Malcolm's goal in life, is to continue researching cases pertaining to the strange world of UFOs and the paranormal, and to hopefully provide some answers to account for what at present eludes us.

AUTHOR'S FOREWORD

I've been researching the strange world of the paranormal for over 45 years now, and in that time I have met some wonderful and interesting people, and have been fortunate to hear some wonderful and fantastic and astonishing tales. Needless to say, that in those 45 years, certain stories stick out, and have challenged my way of thinking. Some have proved very traumatic to those who were on the sharp end of the strange phenomena, and the world's media can, at times, be very cruel to people who experience the paranormal, and this is why many hundreds (and probably thousands) don't come forward and relate their own personal experiences. Thankfully some do, and back in November of 2011, a lady made herself known to me and relayed some horrific childhood and ongoing paranormal experiences that not only affected her life, but that of her daughter as well. That lady was Patricia Hession. This book I hope, will show you the reader, the traumatic events that both Patricia and her daughter Amanda have experienced all their lives. At times the reader may question and dismiss the accounts as being too weird and 'off the wall', but that's the thing with the paranormal, it is *'OFF THE WALL'* The accounts in this book will strain your credulity, of that, make no mistake! It may read like fiction, but I can assure you the reader, that what you are about to read, 'did' happen. A lot of people don't realise how devastating some aspects of the paranormal can be, and sadly, there is not a lot of support out there for people who are experiencing these events to turn to. And when some people turn to officialdom to seek answers and help, many times doors will be closed in their face. Some sceptics may see the accounts in this book as imaginary, and are either made up, or at the very least both Patricia and Amanda were hallucinating and in not full awareness of their senses. If that were the case, then it is my opinion that this would be a global psychosis of immense proportions of which psychiatry would find hard to understand, but equally it would be of great interest to study! Needless to say, I don't think being plagued be Demons is a global psychosis. Yes of course there are situations in which some people are deluded. They may see things under drugs, or they may not be in their right mind, either though a medical episode or a head injury. That may well be, but one has to recognise the seriousness of incidents and experiences that I feature in this book. Not only were mother and daughter being subjected to demonic alarming events in the house, but they have also encountered UFOs and have been abducted by strange 'beings'. You, the reader, may come to your own conclusion at the end of the book. You may share in the grief and desperation of both Patricia and Amanda, or you may dismiss the accounts out of hand. One thing is for sure, you cannot ignore the dramatic events that both mother and daughter have experienced throughout their lives. But it leaves the big question, WHY? Why does this happen to some people? Well I'll share my opinions on that very question at the end of this book, they are only my speculations, and some might dismiss them out of hand, which of course is their right. But I hope at the very least, that after finishing this book, you the reader will come away with a different mind set in regards to accounts of this nature. Please note, that in the main, this is Patricia and Amanda's story, it is 'their' text, that builds the bulk of this book. My part of this book, is to comment, and provide my thoughts as to what they have both experienced. Please note, that pseudonym's have been given to certain people in this book, this is to protect their identity. Their real names are on file with the author. So sit back and be aware, that life, is not always what it seems, that's certainly true in the Hession household.

CHAPTER ONE
(Amanda and I)

As stated above, I first became aware of Patricia Hession back in 2011 where we were exchanging e-mails about her ongoing situation of having to deal with paranormal forces in her home. Patricia then placed a statement on my Facebook page, here in part, is what it said.

"Hi, I'm Patricia from Dublin Ireland, and my daughter Amanda and I have been in contact with craft/UFOs and the Grey's in various sizes, Reptilian, very black beings in various sizes. We have also witnessed tall white 'beings', also small 'beings' that resemble blobs of water, and we have also seen many orbs of various colours. There have been flashes of blue, green and red light in and outside our home. We have been abducted throughout our lives since childhood. I am now 45, my daughter Amanda is 20. Amanda was hypnotised here in Monkstown Dublin Ireland, by Master Hypnotist Tim Richards of Total Mind Dynamics. He had to stop her session abruptly, because he was very concerned about her health and state of mind as she was shaking, crying, and retching erratically, and her body temperature dropped. She felt like a corpse".

(Author's Note). I'll mention more about this hypnotic session later.

"Tim mentioned the Grey's, but there was another who spoke to Amanda in riddles through her mind. We also have experienced shadow beings quite regularly, and one we still fear to this day is known as, 'The Hat Man'. I came forward several years ago after my daughter was hypnotised because I feared for her and wanted answers. Malcolm Robinson, was the first to believe me, and he reached out and helped me more than I could ever repay him. He gave me the contacts of

Paranormal investigators and that got the ball rolling, so to speak. Through Malcolm's friends on Facebook, I have made outstanding friends who are researchers, investigators, abductees, contactees, all who have experienced the Paranormal and UFOs I am here through recommendation of Mr. David Sean Pritchard, as my daughter and I have the ability to use our minds through telepathy. We have what we call our 'Sky Family' where we ask these UFOs and Orbs which we see above our back garden and our neighbour's garden, to give us a true sign by illuminating the white light of their craft as they fly overhead so our eyes can focus on them. I do not know who is in these crafts, but we do not fear them. We all get a feeling of pure joy, bliss and love like no other. We get a longing to be with them. My daughter and I say we want to go home, but not sure where home is! I told Malcolm Robinson and others, that I am more than willing to meet up at some time and have polygraphs or whatever tests necessary done to verify that I'm telling the truth. I am open to the military testing me also"

PATRICIA'S EARLY LIFE

I knew that after receiving not only Patricia's Facebook post, but the countless e-mails from her as well, that I just had to get her and Amanda to tell me as much as she possibly could about all of her strange encounters, little did I know at the time, how much she and her daughter had gone through. And nearly every day, since that day in 2011, Patricia would e-mail me with information that she had recalled and indeed, was 'still experiencing'! But I needed to get to the start. I needed to know a little bit about herself and her early life, so what follows is (in her own words, with a little editing) how it all started for her.

MY EARLY LIFE

"Before I even begin, I would sincerely like to thank my dear friend Malcolm Robinson for whom I would not be writing

6

all the accounts that my daughter Amanda and I have experienced, spanning from our childhood to the present day. I was born to a very young gypsy girl in Worcester, Massachusetts on February 1st 1966. I was baptised by my birth mother, Barbara Nicholas and my birth father Paul Houle, as Michelle Nicholas. I was placed into foster care and adopted two years later in 1968 by the only parents that I have been blessed to have in my life, Mr John C. Hession, and Mrs Norah P. Hession, both of Irish Decent, who later told me that I am of Irish, French, and Amazique/Berber decent. I found out that my birth mother and her siblings were put into foster homes. On my adoption papers, it stated my birth grandmother, Eva who was of gypsy decent, suffered from psychosis and she was locked up. My brother Walter and I were separated and put up for adoption, but I found Walter and my birth mother Barbara 7 months after my mom died. Walter was adopted by an Italian family, and is an artist in Astoria, Queens, New York, and is doing very well for himself, we still keep in touch. I hope to finally meet up with him within the next two years. Barbara said that her mother, Eileen, always saw things that drove her insane. Walter, my brother, told me he had bad experiences when he was young. My birth grandfather was a criminal French gypsy who left his family after numerous convictions and joined a travelling circus".

Patricia further stated.

"I was a very unusual child from the start, as my parents would tell me how I was found lying on the floor in my bedroom after my parents had placed me in my cot the night before. They couldn't figure out how I could get out of my cot as the frames were too high for my legs to go over, and the rail was too high for me to reach. My father would say that I could not have climbed out the cot or got through the wooden bars as they were slotted tightly together. My mother said that when I was very young, she'd notice me looking upwards in full concentration and following something, but nothing could be seen. My mother dismissed this, as she herself couldn't see anything. My parents would also come into the room and hear me laughing and speaking in gibberish when no one was

7

around. On another occasion, my parents found me walking with one arm raised up, as if someone/thing was holding my hand. Now as I got older, my parents feared for my life as everything was well secured in the family home but sometimes I would be found outside. I fell down the stairs many times, but I kept telling my parents that I was 'pushed'. I started kindergarten at five years of age, and I would frighten the children by asking them "Do the funny little men visit you at night when your mommy and daddy and sleeping"? My parents would tell others that it was all my imagination, or that I had been dreaming, and they would tell me not to be telling these stories any more. When I was seven, things took a terrifying turn for me. I saw a dark man wearing a hat and long coat who stared at me then vanished"

"When I was 11, we moved into a new home at Watts Street Malden, Massachusetts, U.S.A. My father was a designer and he kept his clothing patterns in the basement. I had gone down there to use a water pick to clean my braces that I had placed over an old sink, when I suddenly got a feeling inside me of being watched. I turned around, and where my father's patterns were hanging, I saw a dark figure of a man hunched down in the corner staring right at me. The figure was wearing a hat and a long coat, he was old in appearance, but when I screamed for my parents he vanished up the stairs before my eyes. My parents later said that I was imagining things and seeing things that were not there. But if it was just my imagination, then why did my father install several large fluorescent lights several months later!"

THE SILVER LAKE INCIDENT

Later that year we went to Silver Lake in New Hampshire for our summer vacation. I had been given permission from my parents to go for a walk on a nature trail with a black girl that I had made friends with, I can't recall her name now. The walk should only have taken us half an hour, 15 minutes there, and 15 minutes back. When we got back to the beach, all hell broke loose. Our parents, people, life guards, and police, everyone

8

was searching for us. We had been gone for over 3 hours! My parents thought that we had drowned or had been taken by some lunatic. The thing is, we believed that we were not gone for that long. Some of you reading this may think that we just wandered off and got lost, well let me tell you, 'we did not'. I remember staying on the dirt track and just stopping for a brief moment to look back at two strange men who wore black suits, black shoes, white shirts, black ties and hats. They did not appear to have any hair on their head (or so it appeared) and they were wearing dark sunglasses. To me, they resembled the marines. They were spotless and in sync with each other. The black girl and I found them very strange and they continued to stare forward at us whilst walking by us as if we weren't there. They never spoke or said "Hi". And I often wondered why they were wearing suits at a holiday camp on such a hot day. Was this 'missing time'? Were these the so called, 'Men in Black'?

MISSING TIME!

"On another vacation, I remember that it was night time and we were driving to up state New York. I was lying down in the back seat of the car watching strange lights in the sky. I then sat up and noticed that there were forests on each side of the road, and my father said to my mother, "What time is it, as my watch has stopped". My mother replied, "You're not going to believe this, but so has mine". My father said that we should have reached a Motel by now. When we finally reached a Motel, I heard my father tell my mother that he just couldn't understand it, why both watches had stopped. Then he said that several hours had passed and things just didn't make sense at all. I mentioned to my parents of seeing strange lights in the sky, but neither of them said anything and we went to sleep. We stayed in this Motel for a few nights, and I remember a loud rattling on the roof. My father thought that it might be racoons, so he went out to have a look. A few minutes passed, then there was a bright red light flashing through the window. For some reason, my mother grabbed me and we were ducking down on the floor. And then my father arrived back and was startled looking at us, nothing was said".

9

"Then when I was around 14 or 15 years of age, I went to school on a Friday morning and asked my teacher if we could offer up our prayers for my dad who was very sick in hospital and was going to die. (My father was 'not' sick in hospital at this stage)! On Monday evening, my father arrived home and we went to his appointment with Doctor Goldstein, a heart specialist, as my father had had a heart attack a year or so previously. I remember at that time lying in bed with my mother and telling her that my father would die and she called me evil. Now, he did not die back then, but he was sent into hospital by Doctor Goldstein for tests. On the Tuesday night, they were transferring him to the Lawrence Memorial Hospital, to the Massachusetts General Hospital where he suffered a massive heart attack and died in the early hours of Wednesday morning. My mother did not wake me up to tell me that she had received a call from the hospital to tell me that he had died, and so she was surprised when after I woke up in the morning, I told her that he had died. I could see the look of shock on her face. I will never ever forget that look on her face. My mother didn't speak to me when I said this, I guess she was in shock. Later that day, my father's cousin, Jack Martyn told me that he had died, and I just said that I already knew".

BACK TO IRELAND

"My mother brought my father's body back home to Ireland and had him buried in Glasnevin Cemetery in Dublin in January 1980. I moved here to Raheny Dublin in 1982, and lived with my cousin Francis and her husband Sean. My mother moved here a year later and lived with her sister, my aunt Eileen, until she bought this home that I am currently living in from my cousins in 1984. In the first few months of living here, I felt uneasy, but not frightened. When living with my cousin, I felt very uneasy at night as if someone was watching me. I could feel pressure on my feet that slowly ran up my body, and my cousin's young son Darren, said that he had seen a man wearing a hat at the end of his bed, but for some strange reason, I thought that he had seen my father's

10

spirit. I had blocked out what had happened to me in America. I never once felt peace in this home. I was always uneasy and restless and searching for answers as to what was going on. Why are they here? Who and what are they? What do they want? 'me', 'us'? "

"My next door neighbour's son James, asked me one day why my daughter wants me to hold her hand going to sleep at night, is she seeing the old man? He told me his sister May, used to see him too. My daughter, aged two at the time, also saw many strange things, from women, coloured lights, and the 'man'. They seem to be coming more frequently now than ever before. We are paralysed with fear in bed, and an intense rush of heat enters our body. Then there was the time when our small dog broke his leg, so he slept upstairs with us. My daughter and I awoke to hear running back and forth on our bedroom floor, but the dog was fast asleep".

"Malcolm, you are thinking who am I speaking of. All I can say to you is, many 'beings,' 'spirits, 'entities'. I've seen orbs and flashes of lights in various colours. I've seen aliens from the Greys to Reptilians. I've seen tall white beings and others that resemble blobs of water that you just see an outline of. I've seen shadow beings, demonic beings, I've also seen men women and children with various colours around them. Then there is 'HIM', the one that puts a dreaded fear inside you, like no other, 'THE HAT MAN'

WHEN THINGS WENT OFF THE SCALE?

"I would say from the year 1989 onwards, was when things went off the scale. There then began a series of visitations and experiences with the paranormal that has haunted my daughter and I to this day. Just about two months before I was pregnant, I was sleeping in my room, when I woke up and noticed that my feet and legs felt cold. Then I suddenly heard scratches on my bedroom door. All of a sudden my duvet was pulled over my head and I was being held down and my legs were forced open. I called out for my mother but found that I couldn't speak. Something felt like it was copulating with me, but different, in a kind of floaty feeling way. When my daughter was a toddler,

11

she would not go to sleep unless my mother or I held her hand. One time when I was watching television with my mother, I felt an urgency to go up and check on my daughter Amanda. Amanda was sitting up in bed staring at something at the end of the bed, and it was then, at that precise moment, that I began to fear for her life".

HAD THE ANGELS SAVED AMANDA!

"When Amanda was around nine or ten, it would have been the year when I left her father, we were travelling around Ireland, and on our first night we stayed in the Galway Ryan Hotel, (Now known as the Connacht Hotel) After checking in, Amanda wanted to go to the children's pool, but before we were allowed to go to the adjacent indoor pool, I had to sign both of our names in and out at the desk beside the entrance and exit. When we entered, we found that the childrens pool was empty and closed off. The lifeguard who was on duty, said Amanda could use the jacuzzi as the pool was deep, and we told her that Amanda couldn't swim. As I walked down the length of the pool, there was a family of four, two adults and two children of Amanda's age. They were in a section of the pool that was bubbling, so Amanda stepped down into the water, but as she walked over towards the children, she went straight down into a six foot drop as she was on a ledge, we didn't know when your feet actually touched the bottom of the ledge. There are sensors on the ledge that create bubbles. Don't get me wrong, I can swim, but I froze in fear. I could see Amanda looking up at me from beneath the water with her hands up, trying to fight for her life, not knowing or understanding why I was just standing there, staring at her, and not saving her. All of a sudden, as her eyes began to roll back in her head, the man saw the sheer expression of fear and alarm in my face and swam under and gave Amanda to the lady who was now on the ledge. I quickly grabbed a hold of Amanda, but she didn't need resuscitation which was indeed a miracle. Another man who was swimming near the lifeguard, got out of the pool and came towards us, along with the life guard to ensure that Amanda was alright. I said thank God that man and woman was there

12

to save her or I would have been bringing her home in a box. They both looked at me bewildered and said in unison, "What man and woman"? I said, "The family with the two children"! And the lifeguard said, "But we are the only ones in here, just us four"! I immediately looked all around me, and the area was completely empty, so I rushed into the changing rooms expecting the family to have been in there, but it was completely empty. When we left the pool and had to sign out, I noticed two more signatures right beneath our printed names, but not in my hand writing. Someone had written our names to sign out! Believe what you want, but Amanda and I both believe that they were angels".

DIFFERENT FROM OTHER PEOPLE!

"Then there was another night, we were lying in bed, when Amanda said, "Mam do you feel that"? I did indeed. I felt tremendous pressure on my feet, paralysing me as it slowly crawled up my body suffocating me. Then I felt my throat tightening up, then I suddenly blacked out. Malcolm, this is now happening to Amanda. After that night, Amanda started telling me of other things that were happening as well, which consisted of 'beings' that she was also seeing. I, unlike my own parents, told her that I believed her, as it had been happening to me from an early age. Both Amanda and I, knew from an early age that we were different from most people. We are loners, only having a few close friends. I always felt that we did not belong here. We like the company of people on our terms, so to speak, we can do without most people in our lives. We prefer nature if that makes sense. We feel some of it has to do with our own bloodline,(whatever that may be?) We feel at times, we are more than the body we occupy. Reincarnation, yes, quite possible, but we are more Spiritual, more one with God. We both have an uncanny way with animals, more so than people. Both of us were bullied in school because of our differences and for knowing and seeing things that they didn't".

DEVIL'S SECRET SERVICE

*"When my daughter was 17, in 2007, things began escalating, as my mother wasn't well with what her G.P. thought was a bad sinus infection. This went on for several months. I don't know why, but I took Amanda up to bed and I was very angry with God, and I told him that I wanted a true sign to confirm what both Amanda and I knew, that my adopted mother had cancer, a brain tumour, and that she was going to die soon. From 12:00pm till 3:00pm, our built in wardrobes rattled. Wind circulated around us in our bed and it sounded like people were running back and forth in the attic. The following morning, I brought my mother to see a different doctor for a second opinion, and Doctor Coleman, placed her hand on my mother's face and sent her straight into hospital to see an oncologist. The hospital diagnosed that my adopted mother did indeed have a brain tumour. I cared for her at home, then one night I was in bed, before my mother died, Amanda was fast asleep next to me, when in her sleep I heard her say the words, **"Devils Secret Service"**! At least I hope it was her! I woke up, and threw my arm over her where she then woke up quite startled. At this point we both witnessed to our astonishment, our bedroom door throw itself open, with nobody at all to be seen. At this point I said, "Get the f**k away from my daughter, leave, get out"! How me managed to sleep after that I don't know, but we both slept until the morning. About a week or two before my mother passed (she had been in a hospital bed in our front sitting room for a few months) I began saying the Divine Mercy prayer asking for a safe journey home for her soul. At that point, my neighbours, Paul and his wife Rita Sullivan, came in to see my mother. No sooner were they in the house when the television began switching itself on and off, and then it began flicking through all channels, 'it wasn't even switched on'! Indeed the remote control was on the table. That was enough for Paul, he was off. And if that wasn't enough, there then appeared a blue light, and the figure of a spirit which rose above the television and then sat behind Rita on my mother's sick bed. At this point, Rita got our Holy water and started to throw it around our room and also on us. When she*

had finished, she sat back on the bed and said to me, "Is there a spirit or something behind me"? We told her that yes there was, but not to be afraid as it was Holy. I then told Rita that both Amanda and I had seen this beautiful blue being in an illuminated electric blue long dress, the blue colour of a flame. She had reddish golden hair and wore a crown of flowers. She was seven foot tall and hovered at the curtains behind out television, but now she was next to Rita. Rita kept telling me that she was scared and could I ask it to please 'go away', which she eventually did. Now I say lady, but I'm really not sure as to who or what this 'being' was. Part of me says an angel, and the other part of me says, our Blessed Lady because she is always crowned with flowers whenever she has appeared through time. Also, during the time leading up to my mother's death, Amanda and I saw many flashes and streaks of light of vivid blue and emerald green in our bedroom and our sitting room. Now getting back to when I was praying the Novena to the Divine Mercy"

(Author's Note) The Novena is usually recited at the hour of great Mercy, the three o clock hour, but it can be said anytime)

"A bright green image appeared on the dark blank screen of our television. At first I thought it was a monk, a hooded monk, and I asked the image, "Who are you"? The image held a bright red square in its hands and I knew that my prayers regarding my mother's soul safe journey home was indeed answered. This image was of Saint Maria Faustyna Kowalska".

(Author's Note). Wikipedia tells us that, and I quote.

Maria Faustyna Kowalska (was born Helena Kowalska on the 25th August 1905, and died, 5th October 1938) also known as Saint Maria Faustyna Kowalska of the Blessed Sacrament and popularly spelled Faustina, was a Polish Roman Catholic nun and mystic. Her apparitions of Jesus Christ inspired the Roman Catholic devotion to the Divine Mercy and earned her the title of 'Secretary of Divine Mercy'. Throughout her life,

15

Kowalska reported having visions of Jesus and conversations with him, which she noted in her diary, later published as *'The Diary of Saint Maria Faustina Kowalska Divine Mercy in My Soul'*. Her biography, submitted to the Congregation for the Causes of Saints, quoted some of the conversations with Jesus regarding the Divine Mercy devotion. At the age of 20 years, she joined a convent in Warsaw. She was later transferred to Plock and then to Vilnius, where she met Father Maurice Stevens, who was to be her confessor and spiritual doctor, and who supported her devotion to the Divine Mercy. With this priest's help, Kowalska commissioned an artist to paint the first Divine Mercy image, based on her vision of Jesus. The Roman Catholic Church canonized Kowalska as a saint on the 30th April 2000. The mystic is classified in the liturgy as a virgin, and is venerated within the church as the 'Apostle of Divine Mercy'.

Patricia continues with her account.

GYPSY HERITAGE

"I would also like to add here as I have just remembered, as soon as we arrived home from the hospital after my adopted mother had been diagnosed with a brain tumour, she sat down on her bed and handed me a metal box which contained my adoption records and information. She then told me to get in touch with the Department of Social Services in Farnsworth Street Boston and find my biological mother Barbara, as I may find some answers to my questions on what she and my father could not answer. My mother told me that Barbara and my grandmother had psychic abilities, and were known as 'wise women' of gypsy heritage, and that she and my father believed that I had these abilities in my blood. She said that they did not want to acknowledge this in light of all the strange occurrences that had been going on around my daughter Amanda and I because they were frightened by it. This made a lot of sense to me now, and I could fully understand why she called me 'evil'. Not only did I tell her that my father would die, (has died) but I also told her that my aunt Eileen and my uncle Kevin, as well as my uncle Michael and my uncle Brendan, had passed away

16

'before' she received the news herself. Now before I contacted Barbara, my birth mother, I was on the phone to Sheila Frankel from Social Services, and just at the point when she was giving me information, Amanda suddenly pipped up and said, "I have a brother, and his name is Walter. Well, after I had received the contact details on Barbara, I asked Sheila what about my brother, and she said that Walter, my brother, had been searching for me for over a year!"

"Now when I got round to calling my birth mother Barbara, she told me that when she was younger she was placed into foster care, along with her siblings who were later separated from her then adopted. Barbara said that her own father was a convicted felon who later abandoned his family to join a travelling circus. Her mother then turned to drinking, but eventually sought help to get her life back on track. But being an Irish gypsy, she was not educated, and being illiterate she tried her best to answer the questions asked by the medical profession and others. Barbara told me that her mother was devastated when they diagnosed her with some form of psychosis and had her institutionalised. Barbara went onto say that one of the questions they asked was, "Do you see anything"? "Do you hear anything"? as the women in Barbara's mother's family were known as 'wise women' (some would say Witches), that they had gifts of psychic abilities and were always surrounded by spirits through their ancestral bloodline. Surprisingly, only a few men folk had a connection to the spirit world, and Barbara believes that her mother answered yes to all those questions, not knowing the outcome that would follow. She confirmed that my side of the family were French, and that my grandfather's were Amazique/Berber gypsies. Barbara went on to tell me that my biological father, Paul Houle, was the son of her foster parents, and when she got pregnant at 15, it was decided that they would place me into foster care until they could care for me. A year later, in 1967, she gave birth to my brother Walter, who was also placed into foster care, and it wasn't until later that we were put up for adoption. Barbara said that she was removed from her father and the foster home, and sent to live in another foster home. She went onto marry, but many years later she got divorced and

17

never had any more children. She never saw or heard from my father Paul again after that day she was taken away. She said that the man she married, Andrew Chu, was a good man, but that her heart would always be with my father Paul Houle".

(Author's Note) As we can see from the above, Patricia had a troubled childhood and clearly had a lot going on in her early life. Her family history is also scattered with family members having their own problems and being from a gypsy stock, it would appear that Patricia herself, had inherited *'the gift'*. If she thought that things would eventually quieten down, then she was in for a shock, as the strange events in her life just seemed to continue on a daily basis. In the following chapter, Patricia continues with her early life experiences.

11 year old Patricia saw Hat Man in this house in Malden
Massachusetts USA

Little Apple dolls. Part of Amanda's childhood. Had a life of
their own.

Patricia in the middle, holidaying in New Hampshire, USA.
The year of missing time and UFOs.

Patricia with her mother and father at Clive Street,
Massachusetts, USA.

Patricia's adopted mother and father on Boston Common USA

Patricia's adopted parents. Norah and John Hession in front of
The Prince of Peace Church where Pat was baptised.

Pat's first home, Clive Street, Jamaica Plain, Massachusetts USA. (Ground Floor)

CHAPTER TWO

More Bizarre Experiences

"Now getting back to the strange experiences that began happening more frequently in our home during my mother's illness and thereafter. After the night when my daughter uttered those strange words, "Devil's Secret Service" in her sleep, we started to see flashes and streaks of coloured lights and various coloured orbs. Indeed I have seen many coloured orbs whilst working in elderly people's homes working as a carer in Palliative care. We've had household lights flicking on and off, and then there's been strange knockings, raps, three times in a row on our sitting room and bedroom doors. Our box room door would open, and on one occasion, we awoke to a sweet familiar smell, only to then hear a whoosh and a flapping sound come from the box room alongside a candle that was lit, (we did not light it!) Some of the most bizarre things that both Amanda and I have seen, are the seven foot tall white 'beings' in our bedroom, although I've since found out from Amanda who told me that she was seeing these seven foot tall white 'beings' when she was very young. These 'beings' look human, but in point of fact have 'pure white sparkling skin, like glitter'. They also have long white robes, and long white hair and very long beards. Strangely, we didn't see their eyes. Then we've had the 'Hat Man' followed by the Greys".

(Author's note). For the reader who perhaps is not aware of what Patricia is relating to as the Greys, they are small 'beings', roughly around three and a half to four feet tall, small child like body, with a pear shaped head, with black inky almond shaped eyes. There is no clear sign of any genitalia, and their skin is often reported bluey grey, or sometimes even white. They are usually witnessed in or around what we would call, UFOs, but have also been seen inside the family home of people who claim to have been abducted. Patricia continues)

SO WHO WAS THE PRIEST DRESSED IN THE LONG ROBE?

"We would often find some of our jewellery, clothing and small items had disappeared from our house, and no matter how hard we tried, we couldn't find them. That was until a few days later when they would suddenly appear in the very place that they had been in the first place. All very confusing. As the months progressed, my adopted mother was sent to St Luke's cancer hospital for radiation treatment to try and stop her brain tumour from spreading to her throat, so that she would not haemorrhage and die from chocking and drowning on her own blood. While she was lying in bed in an upstairs room alongside another patient, my mother noticed a Priest at the doorway, so we called him in. He then proceeded to give my mother Holy Communion and blessed both her and us. This Priest then spoke to us telling us not to give in to fear as we were all protected. He put his hand over mine, then over Amanda's head, then he smiled and left the room turning right. No sooner did he leave, then another priest all dressed in black, entered the room and asked my mother if she wanted to receive the Blessed Sacrament. This priest was absolutely shocked when we told him that she had already received it from another priest. At this he asked what did this other priest look like, and which way did he go, for he certainly didn't pass him in the corridor or the stairway he stated. The priest also said that there were only four other rooms for eight more patients on this floor and there was also a conservatory. I told this priest that the other priest was elderly, and was wearing a long robe the colour of which the Cardinals wear, and had some beautiful and intricate lace in pure white throughout it. I also said that he looked very similar to Padre Pio".

(Author's note). Wikipedia tells us, and I quote.
Padre Pio, also known as Saint Pio of Pietrelcina (Italian) Pio da Pietrelcina, born 25th May 1887, died 23rd September

24

1968, was an Italian friar, priest, stigmatist and mystic, now venerated as a saint in the Catholic Church. Born Francesco Forgione, he was given the name of Pius (Italian: Pio) when he joined the Order of Friars Minor Capuchin. Padre Pio became famous for exhibiting stigmata for most of his life, thereby generating much interest and controversy. He was both beatified (1999) and canonized (2002) by Pope John Paul II.

Patricia continues with her account.

"Well needless to say, at hearing this, the priest went pale and took off down the corridor in search of this mysterious other priest. A few minutes passed, and the second priest entered the room looking a little bit worse for wear and calmly said, "You are all truly blessed and left the room. We never ever saw that beautiful lady in blue again that appeared when my mother was near death, nor the apparition image of Saint Faustyna. After my mother had passed away, I was sitting on my bed applying my make up, when I suddenly sensed that someone was near me, however, I couldn't see anything. I wasn't scared, and I asked out loud, "Who are you"? I said this a few times. I then found myself saying, "Who am I"? The answers I received were, 'Anu, Anu Char, then Innana, followed by Ishtar. After searching the internet, I found out that Anu is known as a Sky God, God of the Heavens in ancient Sumerian Babylonian text.

(Author's Note). I myself decided to check the internet in regards to these names, and here is what I found. The word/name Innana and Ishtar are effectively, the same deity.

From Wikipedia, and I quote.

"Inanna is an ancient Mesopotamian goddess associated with love, beauty, sex, war, justice and political power. She was originally worshipped in Sumer under the name 'Inanna', and was later worshipped by the Akkadians, Babylonians, and Assyrians under the name 'Ishtar'. She was known as the 'Queen of Heaven', and was the patron goddess of the Eanna temple at the city of Uruk, which was her main cult centre. She was associated with the planet Venus and her most prominent

25

symbols included the lion and the eight-pointed star. Her husband was the god Dumuzid (later known as Tammuz) and her sukkal, or personal attendant, was the goddess Ninshubur (who later became conflated with the male deities Ilabrat and Papsukkal). Inanna was worshipped in Sumer at least as early as the Uruk period (c. 4000 BC – c. 3100 BC) During the post-Sargonic era, she became one of the most widely venerated deities in the Sumerian pantheon, with temples across Mesopotamia. The cult of Inanna/Ishtar, which may have been associated with a variety of sexual rites, was continued by the East Semitic-speaking people (Akkadians, Assyrians and Babylonians) who succeeded and absorbed the Sumerians in the region. She was especially beloved by the Assyrians, who elevated her to become the highest deity in their pantheon, ranking above their own national god Ashur. Inanna/Ishtar is alluded to in the Hebrew Bible and she greatly influenced the Ugaritic Ashtart and later Phoenician Astarte, who in turn possibly influenced the development of the Greek goddess Aphrodite. Her cult continued to flourish until its gradual decline between the first and sixth centuries AD in the wake of Christianity. Inanna appears in more myths than any other Sumerian deity. She also had a uniquely high number of epithets and alternate names, comparable only to Nergal. Many of her myths involve her taking over the domains of other deities.

MEETING BEVERLEY BROOKS

Now that Patricia and Amanda had moved to Ireland, they quickly made friends with a number of local people, even although, as she would tell you herself, she still prefers her own company. In 2007, she was to meet a woman who would have a dramatic influence on her life. And here is how it all started.

"It was a few days after my mother's funeral, so that would have been in September 2007, when I was in my local post office when people that knew my mother started to gather around me and were talking about her. Now this was getting all too much for me, and I began crying. With that, a woman

*called Beverley took me aside. I knew Beverley from years ago
as her youngest son, Steven, and his father Alec lived across the
road from me. Alec had initially introduced us way back in
2003 but we never really got to know each other after that time.
Beverley did not know my mother, but was extremely
sympathetic and kindly said, "Come back to mine's and I'll
stick the kettle on". So, owing to her kindness, I went. As soon
as Beverley opened the door, I suddenly felt that all too familiar
feeling of fear. I looked up her stairs towards the landing and
froze. 'He' was there! Beverley and her son Steven, who was
five years old at that time, both knew that I had seen 'Him,' the
dreaded 'Hat Man'. Beverley kept asking me "What do you
see"? "Tell me, tell me what you see"? I said nothing, but
'she knew' as her son had previously said to me that the bad
man that's in our house, is also in yours as well, and you will
see him later. I told Beverley that there was evil in her house
and quickly left. Believe me when I say that evil was indeed in
her house! Tim Richards, a friend of mine who is also a
hypnotherapist, also said it, and he would not go inside to help
her. On one occasion, he only stayed outside Beverley's house
for five minutes, as he did not like the feeling and vibes and the
negativity that he was getting from standing outside her house.
He even had this sensation when he was going up her road
towards her home".*

*"Some time later, I bumped into Beverley and Steven in our
local shopping centre and invited them both back to my house
for lunch. As soon as they entered my home, Beverley was
drawn to and fascinated by, an oil painting of my mother in her
wedding dress. Steven then said out loud, that my father was
here to which took me by surprise. So I challenged him by
going upstairs where I found an old black and white
photograph of my father as a young boy wearing his
confirmation clothes sitting in rows of his class with around 40
other boys. I then asked Steven to point out my father, in the
photograph, and much to my amazement, as well as Amanda's,
Steven pointed his finger into the middle row and moving his
finger slowly back and forth, back and forth, said, "One two
three, one two three, then pointed straight to my father! That
night after they had gone home, I went out to my kitchen to*

27

make a cup of tea, I had just opened the sitting room door only to see 'Him' 'Hat Man', crouching down on the third stair in my hall. He turned his head sideways, stood up, and glared at me. But this time I wasn't scared. I quickly ran up my stairs saying, "Who are you? What do you want"? But just at this moment, he suddenly turned into a dark blackish grey smoke and vanished through the trap door in my bathroom, up into the attic. My friend Beverley said that she was a medium, and that both her and her son Steven were gifted. She said Amanda and I are stronger and more gifted because we have lots of spirits, and beings around us and that 'we' complete her triangle.

(Author's Note) It is interesting to note, that Patricia also saw the 'Hat Man' appear in her friend's house and found out that her new friend Beverley and her son Steven, were both psychic and could see and hear things just like Patricia and Amanda. Indeed, little did Patricia know at this time, that things were to get even stranger!

"Let me make it perfectly clear, that throughout my life, we have had our home blessed by priests and many others. From Mormon Ministers to a Druid. The priests prayed with us and blessed each room, sprinkling Holy water. Then they placed their hands on our heads and we all prayed. Then the priests spoke in Latin over us and blessed our heads and palms of our hands in the sign of the cross with Holy Chrism. We've also had a Shaman and a Buddhist Monk. We've also had a member from the Hare Krishna sect come along, and also a Jewish Rabbi. We've had White Witches, both Pagan and Catholic, attend our home. And here in our house, we have numerous Holy medals and blessed relics. We also have Holy water and blessed salt. We have lavender and white sage and numerous crystals and yet 'they' still come. During this time, I saw a lot of Beverley, as I was intrigued by her gifted son, and also the fact that Beverley claimed (and still claims to this day,) to be a Spiritual Medium. On the other side, Beverley would say that Amanda and I were the circles inside her triangle! I asked what she meant by that phrase. She replied that 'our' energies are complete when we are all together"

28

THE OUIJA BOARD AND THE CALLING OUT FOR DEMONS!

"Now, Amanda and I have never used, and will 'never use', an Ouija Board, but Beverley, along with her son and one of her daughter's did, and quite regularly too! One day, Amanda and I were invited over to Beverley's for dinner but we got more than we bargained for! I knew something else might happen, so I decided to take along some Holy water and a Blessed Cross and some Holy medals. Upon entering her home, we found Beverley sitting at a table with her children. We all sat around her table which was a round heavy and very solid wooden one, which sat in the corner near her fireplace. Beverley and her daughter approached the table with an empty glass, and proceeded to place the glass, upside down, in the centre of the table. Next Beverley and her daughter placed two pieces of paper on either side of the glass next to them, after which, both Beverley and her son Steven held hands. I looked at Amanda, Amanda looked at me. Then Beverley started asking the question, "Is anybody there"? As both of them placed a finger on the glass. Beverley kept asking them to 'come forward' and answer some questions. Beverley then surprised us both by saying, "Patricia and Amanda have loads of questions they want answered. And then it all started to get a bit more serious and bizarre, because Beverley then started to call upon the names of Demons, Satan, Lucifer, Beelzabub and Dracos. Both Amanda and I at this point shouted out "NO, we can find our own answers". I quickly jumped up from the table and said very loudly, "Ay nighe hay nin nighe achmed heady". I said these words over and over. I did not know what I was saying, and I am not sure if that's how you spell them, but a Jesuit priest later told me that I was speaking in ancient Aramaic and calling on protection from the Lord"

(Author's Note): Upon looking at Wikipedia to find out more about this language, it stated the following, and I quote.

29

The Aramaic language belongs to the Northwest group of the Semitic language family, which also includes the Canaanite languages, such as Hebrew, Edomite, Moabite, and Phoenician, as well as Amorite and Ugaritic. Aramaic languages are written in the Aramaic alphabet, which was derived from the Phoenician alphabet. One of the most prominent variants of the Aramaic alphabet, still used in modern times, is the Syriac alphabet. The Aramaic alphabet also became a base for the creation and adaptation of specific writing systems in some other Semitic languages, thus becoming the precursor of the Hebrew alphabet and the Arabic alphabet.

Patricia Continues.

"I began holding my daughters hand and Beverley's little son Steven's hand, when all of a sudden, a gust of wind came swirling down from her fireplace, and then everyone started saying the words that I had just said. I don't know to this day what those words mean. "I later asked my uncle, Father Dominic Hession who was an exorcist about this séance, but he did not acknowledge it. Now I do not remember what happened at this point, but Amanda told me that there was a bright illuminating glow that surrounded me, and that I looked much younger. I should point out, that when this particular event happened, ie, speaking these strange words, I was in my mid 40's. Anyway, Steven and Amanda, all held hands and started repeating these words along with me. At this point, we all saw a large blue orb come out of my side and chase after a bright red orb onto the stairs. As soon as this happened, I threw Holy water over everyone, at which point the table started shaking and a strong force of wind came out of her fireplace. Then, a smokey substance, similar to dry ice, come out of the wall where they were all sitting. I prayed, and then cursed at them and left. My relationship with Beverley changed after that, and not for the better, but we still spoke and she still came round to my house"

INVISIBLE FOOTSTEPS AND RIPPLING BED COVERS!

"Many days, weeks, then months passed by, during which both Amanda and I were terrorised by negative 'beings' in our home. One day Amanda was in town, I was back at home watching the television when that dreaded feeling came over me again, but this time, it was during the daylight and I could actually hear, erratic whispering to my left hand side but I was too frightened to turn my head and look. I just fixed my eyes on a small Holy picture of Jesus, then felt a hot tingling sensation throughout my body. If this wasn't bad enough, I then felt a big blow to my chest, as if someone had punched me. At this point I must have fell asleep, as I awoke several hours later when I heard Amanda opening the front door. Things got steadily worse. At night we could both sense evil as we went to bed, and we heard the noise of running footsteps in the attic again. Not only that, we also heard footsteps running up and down our staircase and also across our bedroom floor, yet no one could be seen! Whilst this was going on, our wardrobe would creak, and we would hear three knockings in sequence. This was soon followed by our bed shaking and our covers on the bed making a rippling movement. I had Amanda sleeping next to me since she was a baby, so that was one small comfort and although these paranormal occurrences are consistent, we feel safer together".

"It was Halloween time, and a year since my mother had died, (2008) I was in the kitchen tidying up when all of a sudden I heard a loud crackling sound. I then spotted a greenish orb accompanied by a rusty brown orb going straight through my back door which is made of glass. Again I don't know why, but I reached out my hand to touch it, whereupon the sound got louder and the orbs grew larger than my head. I screamed out in fright and shouted for Amanda, but it just suddenly vanished".

SOME OF OUR UFO AND ORB SIGHTINGS.

"Amanda and I would often go out into our back garden and star gaze, as we love looking at the night sky. Now as it happens, our back garden became a focal point for many strange and awe inspiring events that still take place today. One day whilst we were outside, we observed some amber coloured balls of light, like party sparklers but they have an intelligence and can move about in synchronicity with each other. They were seen by a friend of mine, Margaret Graham as well. Sometimes I call on them in God's name and between one and seven will appear. We felt that they had intelligence. The first three we saw, flew in sync from the left hand side, and then went above my next door neighbour's tree. They then floated and hovered above our garage, and slowly turned, while floating into an arch position, then they completely vanished in front of our eyes. Then there was the last one who just had to be different. This 'being', as I now call it, flew in front of my neighbour's tree, not over it. It then flew forward in front of my garage at the same level and height as my head. Then it moved up over the garage and decided to stay a while. I was so happy. We felt a pure love like no other from these 'beings'. No fear at all, just a deep connection with them and I call them our 'Sky Family'. After a while, it also flew in an arch and disappeared. We have seen one or two on different occasions since, as did Violet, one of my neighbours. On other occasions, we would see streaks of blue, green and white light appear in our garden, as well as in our home, and our experiences with our 'Sky Family', the Greys, the Demonic 'beings' we now consider normal for us, and yes, that also includes the 'Hat Man' as Amanda and I have both realised that for whatever reason, these 'beings', 'Demons' and 'Spirits', were a part of us, and no matter how many priests and ministers and others whose help we sought along with countless bottles of Holy water, Blessed Relics, Holy Medals, was just not going to get rid of them so we accepted that they will always be around".

WEIRD FINGERS!

"I should also tell you that Amanda and I, along with my brother Walter, used to do something weird with our fingers. We would be deeply engrossed in conversation with my daughter Amanda, and whilst talking, we would position our fingers in a way that resembled the eyes of the Greys, but hold a conversation as if we are talking and something is answering us back"!

"Now its been two years since my mother passed, and the year of 2009 I will never forget, as our visitations and abductions were taking place more regularly, but we could remember them much more clearly. I had just made friends with Beverley again, and Beverley went on to say that she now understood why I had reacted as I did that awful day in her home, (The Seance) and that this was all behind us now, and that we can move forward, moreover, we were 'all connected' through our past lives. Now she had me intrigued, and Amanda was now interested but still very cautious. I asked her what did she mean by this? and both she and her son Steven began to tell us about three recurring dreams that they both had. Now the thing is, I had three recurring dreams that kept coming back over the years since my childhood, and here's the thing, Amanda had the 'exact same dreams' when she was a child. Not only that, my brother Walter, has one of our recurring dreams. I then asked Beverley how did she know about these recurring dreams and I asked her to tell me about them. The following is what she said to us".

FIRST DREAM: "Amanda and I are taken into a large white marbled room by men wearing black and red hooded robes who are chanting something. In the dream, she can see a large black Pentagon on the floor with candles around it within a gold circle that framed and outlined the Pentagon. Amanda and I were both lying down on the star, my feet beside Amanda's head and vice versa. Above us, was a mosaic glass domed window with some sort of gold or brass chain with a pointed pendulum attached. These robed men were all gathered around us, but there was one man, in a dark purple robe, who moved forward towards us".

SECOND DREAM: "This is the one we shared with Walter, my brother. We are not on this Earth, but on a red planet, similar to Mars. I am in a temple or a Royal dwelling, there is white stone all around and there is a sand pit. There are large round clay dishes which contain fire which are sitting on some steps inside this building. There are statues which look Egyptian, but they are not in black. I can somehow see outside, and I see an alien craft which is burning trees and structures with some kind of laser beam. In this dream, I am trying to find this young nobleman who in reality is my brother Walter, and also a noblewoman who is my daughter Amanda, to safety through a secret corridor. We are all dressed in white robes and have jewelled broaches holding the robe together at the shoulder. We are all barefoot and have jewelled bracelets on our upper arms. I am a high priestess according to Walter and Amanda".

THIRD DREAM: "I am standing on a hill, and the sea is in front of me, and to my right I can see a city which is burning. I am surrounded by people who are screaming and crying. I am raising my hands up to the sky where electricity is flowing out from my hands in a bluish colour as I am trying to stop Satan who is in another spaceship which is battling in the sky".

THE ROOM FILLED WITH A BRIGHT EMERALD GREEN LIGHT!

"After Beverley and Steven told us all about 'OUR' dreams, she said that all these dreams were past lives, but that one of them, was both past and a future yet to come. Both Amanda and I knew straight away, that it was the third dream that was both. In the months that followed this conversation, Amanda had to be admitted into Beaumont Hospital in Dublin to have her gall bladder removed, as at this point she was extremely ill. The doctors told us that she had an infection in her gall bladder called cholecystitis and couldn't perform surgery until the

34

infection had cleared. I was given permission to take Amanda down to the Chapel which upon entering was empty of people. We then sat down to pray, and after I had searched for some Holy water to bless Amanda with to keep her safe, I noticed a door behind the alter and decided to knock on it. I then pulled on the handle but it was locked. I then took Amanda back up to her ward and said goodnight and that I would see her in the morning. The following morning, I arrived at the hospital to find Amanda's surgeon waiting for me after he had completed his rounds. He had some of his team with him, but his face said it all! I just knew that it wasn't good news. He told me that Amanda was now much worse than he initially thought, and on top of everything else, she now had pneumonia. At this point he reached for my hands, and clasped them in his, and said that he would do the very best that he can, but her chances were 50-50. At this I rushed into the hospital and went to Amanda's ward and she told me that a priest had given her a small bottle of Holy water. She showed me this little plastic bottle, and it was shaped in the image of our blessed Virgin Mary. It was a clear bottle, outlined in blue. Later that night, I returned home and a few hours later the doctor phoned to say that they couldn't wait any longer to perform the surgery and that Amanda needed the surgery 'now'. Needless to say, I was distraught and crying, I was worried sick beyond belief, and I remember telling God that I do not want you to take her, but if it was his Holy will, then to keep her safe from harm out of this world, and guide her home. For some strange reason, I played a song called Guardian Angel by the Red Jumpsuit Apparatus, and then I forwarded it onto Amanda, as it resonated with me as being 'her Guardian Angel'. At this point, and all of a sudden, my sitting room filled up in a bright emerald green light. I immediately knew that Amanda's surgery had been a success and that she would be alright. I cried and thanked God, my own Angels, Saints, and my Sky Family".

THE MAN WHO SPOKE IN RIDDLES.

"During September 2010, I was admitted to hospital, myself in severe pain with my own gall bladder and was in hospital preparing for surgery. Whilst there, my daughter had her most terrifying experience. What happened was, the following day after I was admitted to hospital, Amanda arrived to see me but I somehow knew that something bad had happened, as I had this feeling the night before, but I didn't want to call or text her as she would worry more. Amanda proceeded to tell me that she was just settling into bed when a 'man' approached her at the side of her bed. He spoke in riddles, and placed something like a mask over her face. She grabbed his arm and cannot remember any more. She then somehow managed to get back to sleep, but upon wakening, she was shocked to see a small Grey in bed beside her! After I came out of hospital, I arranged for Amanda to meet with Tim Richards, the hypnotherapist to get hypnotised. Under hypnosis, she said that when she grabbed this 'man' who had suddenly appeared at the side of her bed, he felt like the silicone chicken fillets inside a bra. During her hypnosis, she was hysterical. Her body was shaking, she had erratic breathing, and she felt freezing cold. Amanda also started recalling under hypnosis, her encounters with the Greys. Tim had to stop the therapy because he was worried about her. But he said, "Something did happen to her". he definitely believed her. Indeed, he further stated that yes indeed, the Greys 'ARE' behind our abductions along with something more sinister! Tim stated that there was no need to put Amanda through any more sessions because of her state of health. I myself have never been hypnotised, but I remain open to it should the need arise".

PLAYING WITH THE OUIJA BOARD AGAIN!

"Then there was the day when Beverley called to say that a friend of hers from Wicklow, a man called Jim, was coming over to stay for the weekend, and that he would love to meet Amanda and I. As it turned out, her friend Jim is also a UFO abductee, and has seen many strange things that he would love

to speak to us about. Well, like a fool, I went back over to Beverley's, our relationship was still a bit strained but she was still my friend. No sooner had I sat down on a chair in the living room, than Beverley brought out a glass and placed it firmly in the middle of the table. Steven, her son, then put down the letters of the alphabet and also the words Yes and No on the table. At this I shouted out, "What the f**k are you doing? You gave me your word that you were not involved in this crap any more". At this, she said that she was just trying to prove something to Jim. Well, as soon as Beverley and Jim placed their fingers on the glass and were asking questions, the lights in the house began to flicker. She then told her young son Steven to join them, and to place his finger on the glass to create more energy, at which point she began to ask out loud, 'Who is there with us, please show yourselves'. Again I let loose and said, "You are not a medium, evil works through you. It's Steven who has the gift, and you are abusing it". Beverley's friend Jim then spoke up and said, "But Patricia, you have many gifts, along with your daughter, but are too afraid to use them". Now, I do not want to come across as a hypocrite or contradict myself as I have always stated that both Amanda and I will 'never' partake in any seances and Ouija Boards, and even though I placed my finger of the damm glass, I did so out of good intentions, not to conjure up anything, but to stop it by using my energy, my will, and my faith. I then said to Jim that it ends here, whilst staring at Beverley, much to the amusement of Amanda. By Jesus, I showed them a part of me that even I didn't know I had in me that day. Anyway, as soon as I placed my finger on the glass, I got a very strange tingling feeling. Just then, Beverley said, "Do you feel that. I have never felt that before, have you Steven"? At this, Steven spoke up and said "No, I haven't". Beverley then said to Jim, "Is that energy coming from you"? But just before Jim could answer her, I said, "It's divine energy coming from me". I should state that I have had a blue orb of energy coming from me before. At this, Beverley began stating in an ever increasing demanding voice, that she wanted to ask her questions, and with that, the glass started to move. At first I thought that Beverley was pushing the glass so I closed my eyes, and asked silently in my mind,

"Are you of the Christ Divine"? I asked this question twice, and then asked, "Are you of the Christ consciousness on the third"? Suddenly a horrid putrid and pungent smell entered the room. We looked down at the table, and the glass was moving around the table in all directions. Steven took his fingers off the glass followed by Jim. It then was a force between Beverley and myself. At this point, the table on which the glass was sitting on, started shaking, both Beverley and I were battling against each other, then Beverley asked out loud, "Why did you ask that" at which point the glass that we both had our fingers on, started spinning widely forming a large circle on the table. I then shouted out loud to Beverley, "Are you of the Christ Divine, the Christ Consciousness". Well, no sooner had the words left my lips, than the glass shot off the table and broke into hundreds of pieces. Suddenly a blue orb came out from behind me and went after a dark evil figure which appeared on her stairs. Then a mist similar to dry ice came out of her sitting room wall. The table shook, and lights flickered. Toys were moving around the floor of their own accord. I got up at this point and left the table, and started to move to her stairway as I felt an evil presence near the kitchen dining room door on the right hand side of me. And then a loud growling voice permeated the air saying, "Noooooo" At this point I felt breath on the right hand side of my face and Beverley went pale and we all were shocked and frightened. I then turned round to Beverley and said, "Well there's your answer, it's 'not' Holy, it's 'pure evil" and with that, I took the Holy water and shook it all over the home then left with Amanda".

"I want you to know Malcolm, that being with Beverley did not bring more evil or paranormal activity into our home, it has always been with me since childhood. That said, I do believe that it was enhanced somehow by our energy and curiosity as we spoke about all these weird and strange events that were occurring in and around our family home. The thing is though, the more paranormal events that happened in our home, the more they played on our minds. This of course increased our fears, and we were always on edge on a daily basis. At this point in our lives, we were being plagued by 'Shadow People'.

38

the 'Hat Man' and the Greys, as well as the unusual noises in our home, so you can see how all this made us on edge".

UFO ABDUCTION!

"Not long after that, it was coming up to Christmas, and Amanda and I had just gone up to bed. Amanda had fallen asleep but I was still awake, when all of a sudden, I heard an electrical humming sound coming from above me. I rolled over onto my back, and there, staring back at me, just below the ceiling, was a whirlpool of colours, all swirling above our bed in unison with each other. As I focused on this amazing spectacle, I could see what looked like a hole in the middle of this swirling mass, but more incredibly, this hole penetrated the attic, the rafters, and the roof of the house, and I was now looking up at the night sky! Suddenly, I was blinded by a bright yellow flash that completely filled our room, and both Amanda and I were lifted out of our bed. Amanda was above me, and I desperately tried to grab her to bring her down but couldn't. After that, I don't remember anything else. However that morning when we were both up, Amanda turned round to me and calmly said that both of us had been taken last night by the Greys, and that the Greys had taken me down one corridor, and Amanda was taken down another. Amanda also recalled that we were both stripped naked, and submerged in some kind of liquid. Not only that, Amanda said that when she was looking around this room, she saw tiny Greys and also saw human looking 'things' inside some kind of pink glass vats, all in align with one another"

METALLIC TASTE IN MOUTH

Patricia also recalls another 'being' that she had never seen before who was on the craft with her. This 'being' was between 3 and 4 foot tall, very fat and shaped like the letter S, but with small arms and feet. She stated,

"I do remember trying to fight this being, but I was pulled off him. He was fat, had tiny arms and feet, and a lower lip

39

much bigger than the top. He also had horse like teeth and was 3 feet in height, similar to the small Grey beings. There were also some very tall white slender beings, with long white hair and beards, roughly seven feet tall or taller. We also saw the Greys and other 'beings'. Amanda and I both had a seedy metallic taste in our mouths this morning, Surprisingly, Amanda felt nothing last night".

STRANGE MARKS ON OUR ARMS.

(Author's Note) Most UFO abductees have noticed strange markings on their bodies after they have been returned from an abduction. This is quite common, although these marks are not always the same, and differ quite considerably from person to person. Some UFO Abductees have what's called, 'scoop marks', semi circular markings, either to be found on arms or legs, or some other part of the body. Small dots have also been observed, both singular and grouped, some in triangular patters. These don't always last, and can disappear after a matter of hours, days or weeks. Patricia goes on.

"I remember many times over the years, waking up in the morning and literally vomiting what I thought was blood, to the extent that my mother at that time, took me to hospital where I had a number of tests done and also had a camera put down my throat. Thankfully I was given the all clear and told that I could go home. A few days passed, and Amanda noticed these unusual and mysterious brown dots that just appeared on her right upper arm, they resembled freckles, but they clearly were not. There were five dots that formed an upside down V. It resembles the Chevron above the tomb of Christ. There is one singular dot which appears beneath this. Now, I have a similar one on my left arm, but not as pronounced as Amanda's. We believe they were put there over time as we were not born with them. To be honest, Amanda's markings started to appear after one of her abductions, when she was around 10 years of age. It is interesting that they have not always been there. I have a lot of freckles and small marks on my arms too that seem to just appear from time to time. Something appeared on the top of my

foot in 2000, a very similar design like the Chevron. I know that I was taken on the night before it appeared, but then later I saw the same design at Rosslyn Chapel. I don't know why, but I feel that I am familiar with the design, like I recognise it somehow, but not sure why"?

"I should also mention at this point, that one night both Amanda and I were watching a Sci Fi film on the Greys on television, when all of a sudden Amanda got hysterical, for there on the screen, were large pink vats containing hybrids, exactly what she saw when she was physically abducted. Needless to say, Amanda was really shaken up by this. But getting back to those marks on Amanda. Not long after those marks appeared on Amanda's right upper arm, Amanda had a small round lump that came out of her inner thigh, I have a similar one, but it is on my shin along with, I might ad, several bruises. Malcolm, I cannot recall exactly when most of these sightings and visitations have taken place, as so much activity has been going on to both of us since our childhood and there has been quite a lot of recall that has come to us in bits and pieces and we are trying to put them all together in the jigsaw of our life. As the years have rolled by, we are still seeing what I call our 'Sky Family' above our home, but what I haven't seen for a while, are those amber coloured balls of light (beings!) I really missed them. Anyway, one day I asked out loud if there were any 'beings' of the Christ Divine, The Christ Consciousness, our 'Sky Family' that might be flying overhead, to please give Amanda and myself a 'true sign,' by illuminating a bright white light of their craft as they fly over head so that our eyes can locate and see them. Well, ever since that day, they've been back, and we have seen them lots of times. These craft can fly in any direction, and turn in an instant, then come down low, then hover, then speed off and disappear. Now I best make clear, that I have asked these craft to appear to my friend and her son Steven, and also my other friends, Margaret, Paula and Rose. They have all seen them. I often say to people who are sceptical, just go outside and ask from your heart with good intentions, and I believe they will come and show themselves to you"

41

(Author's Note) When Patricia told me that she and Amanda had been witnessing UFOs, I asked her if she had ever tried to communicate with them, she replied.

"Sometimes I feel we belong to them. I can sometimes communicate and ask them to show me the illuminating white light of their craft in the sky if they are in our atmosphere. On occasion they appear out of nowhere, and go by very slowly, no sound from their craft. The light is dim at first, then there is a brilliant white light, then it dims back down again. Sometimes they flash twice then disappear. I know this all sounds crazy, that is why I am more than willing to undergo a polygraph if required. I don't fear these 'beings'."

"Then there was another night when I was lying in bed playing around with my energy and aura as I am a natural healer, when I noticed a bright white light coming out from the headboard, and it looked as though my arms and hands were being dissolved as they went through this light. Now, not long after that night, both Amanda and I were putting on our pyjamas, when suddenly hundreds and thousands of small illuminating emerald green spirals started to pour over both Amanda and I. These lights, also covered the whole of our bedroom, the ceiling, the walls, the floor, and, would you believe, even under our bed! We were not scared at all, just startled. I had this warm feeling inside of me which consisted of pure love and bliss, the same type of feeling that we both had when we saw the Blue Lady and our Sky Family Craft along with the amber balls of light and many orbs etc"

YOUR GOD HAS NO PLACE HERE!

"I don't know why, but upon seeing the spirals, I recalled the Celestine Prophecy book that was supposed to be fictitious, but to me felt like the truth. After watching a number of films and series on UFOs and the Paranormal, Amanda and I just know that it is not all 'make believe', as we can relate to and have experienced many of these occurrences. I think with films of a Sci Fi nature, we get hidden clues in them. One night, I woke up in the early hours of the morning to go to the toilet,

when I suddenly saw a familiar face from a strange dream that I had many years ago. But instead of a boy that was in the original dream, it was now a man! At first, I thought that someone had broken into our home, but he was there, clear as day, standing in our doorway next to our built in wardrobes. He looked like our picture of Jesus that we have hanging up on a wall here at home, but he had shorter thick black curly hair. He was extremely beautiful, and that is an understatement. I asked him three times, "Who are you?" and on the third time of asking he said, "The Magistrate" then suddenly he disappeared. Now in my dream of some years ago, I was with a beautiful olive tanned skinned boy with thick black short curly hair. We were standing and embracing in each other's arms and I gently kissed his neck. There were others gathered around us wearing dark robes. This boy had his eyes closed and I asked him several times, "Who are you, what is your name"? But he was silent. I then said, "Does God not want you, or allow you to tell me"? At which point he slowly opened his eyes which were violet, and said, "Your God has no place here"!

"To my recollection, a year or two had passed since I saw the man appear in my room, and Amanda and I were watching television, when, we both at the very same time, saw what we can only describe as a 'water blob being'. There were two of them, approximately between two and three feet tall. One was coming out of the fireplace going towards a similar blob at the far wall beside our television, then they just disappeared. As for these blobs themselves, well we could only see a rippled outline as they both were transparent. Then, after a few months had passed from that incident, we started to hear both of our names being called out, it wasn't us, in the sense of calling out to each other. There was nobody in the house, other than Amanda and myself when our names were being called out. Then a large raven started to appear every morning outside my bedroom window and cawed between 06:00 and 07:00am. It was much larger than the others that we have seen around our house. I started to feed him, after which he started to follow me, or would come into my garden when ever he saw me. I was at my local shop which is ten minutes away from my house, and he would crow and chatter, then fly down all excited to see me, *much to the amusement of the passers by. He would then take flight and be waiting for me in my garden when I got home. We also have two cats, one of which is the image of a banshee! One day I was petting it and talking to it, with Amanda looking on, when suddenly it just 'disappeared' in front of our eyes! Needless to say, that most certainly wasn't our cat! Both of our cats see orbs and 'beings' also! Their eyes and head follow something which we can't see. We still have visitations by the Greys, but most experiences during our lives, have been blocked from our memories, either through trauma, or 'Them' not wanting us to remember. And the 'Hat Man' also makes his dreaded appearance along with Shadow Beings from time to time".*

THE DIVINE MERCY OF JESUS PICTURE

"Another evening in the autumn of 2014, Amanda and I were sitting in our front living room watching television and having a cup of tea. It was around 7:00pm. Amanda suddenly noticed our Holy picture of The Divine Mercy of Jesus, hopping about on the top of the mantelpiece and told me to look. The picture then hovered out in mid air, the lower part was still on the mantle above our fireplace. Then it moved out flat, with the picture of Christ's face facing the floor, but still in mid air above the coffee table. With that, we both heard a loud rumbling noise coming from inside our chimney at which point a very large and heavy mirror was literally thrown off the wall. But instead of crashing down between us, it flew 'over' the Divine Mercy of Jesus picture and crashed in shards on the floor with the hook still attached to our wall, and the heavy twine still attached on the mirror. I know and believe this picture, or who it represents, saved us both from getting hurt, as we moved away in time. I said you are not going to frighten me any more, and I swore at it several times. I then said that I told you we are protected by our God. Enough is enough, this is my home, and you are not welcome in it. Then I said, you are always hiding in your spirit form, if you are so powerful, manifest and show me who you truly are. At this point I felt very sick, and nauseous. My head was spinning, and then I felt a hot

44

burning pain, like the one on my hip, but this time three long straight lines appeared on my lower left arm, again no bleeding, even though it had just happened. It looked old, darkish reddy brown, and cleared in a few days. I know this entity is different from the others that we have had over the years. Although we have a dreaded fear of The 'Hat Man', Shadow Beings and some Greys, this one gives me a different feeling, a sensation in my core when it is here. I believe it gets stronger when I challenge it. It wants desires, a challenge to show how powerful it is, and what it can and will do. Yet, it still will not show itself in matter. I think energy is what gives it its power, yet other beings are energy too, but they use theirs differently, and some can and will manifest".

ANOTHER UFO ABDUCTION?

"Then another few months went by and I remember being on a craft again, I'm not sure if this was a dream or reality. I was lying on a bed of sorts, and at each side of me were other people. Everything was bright white. But in front of me was a large black onyx type of window and control panel, and sitting at it, were two reptilian beings. For some strange reason, I wasn't frightened of them as I am with the 'Hat Man' or the Greys. One of the beings had dark green moss like skin, with some kind of markings and patterns. The other being, was a rusty brown colour, with mustard colour markings, both had bright yellow eyes with slits. I also saw some small Greys who were illuminating a white glow, but they were thinner than usual, and there eyes were smaller. I felt something hot being shoved into my leg but I don't have a mark".

"These beings had long tails and three very long fingers on their hands, with another finger at the back, similar to a bird of prey. I then saw, on my left hand side, a beautiful pale skinned girl with long black hair, black eyes but with no white part in the eyes who resembled a human, but I believe she wasn't! She then spoke to me in a highly regal English manner and said "Hello", and that her name was Julia. She was like a porcelain doll! And she had no nipples! She had some sort of white sheet placed over her. We all had this sheet on us and were naked

45

underneath but hers slipped down on occasion, that's when I saw that she had no nipples. She told me that 'they' do not like us talking. There were other tall gleaming white translucent beings, some of whom were bald with blueish eyes, others were all white but human looking with very long white hair and beards. There were also tall Grey's, there as well, but they were all moving in a floating manner just off the floor. Their legs were not moving, yet they were. I remember being taken into a room just off the long corridor on the left. Another long corridor was on the right. To me, the craft resembled the shape of a boomerang, with the controls in front at the V point. Inside the room was a larger floating glass like table, except, the table had strange markings on it and some oval shapes in different sizes. There was also an object above it that looked like a huge rotary part of a razor. Three metallic circular grooved discs attached to something hanging from the ceiling. I could hear a strange electronic buzzing sound, and then I woke up around 01:00am to go to toilet, at which point I smelt the familiar fishy, bleachy smell. I then heard a noise on the stairs, and saw two men wearing black suits. I have seen men in black before, as a child, so I thought I would ask them why 'they' take us? Why do the aliens want us? As they got closer, I saw their faces, and thought Demons. They looked like snakeskin lizards, but there skin was dark moss green with some light creamy brown markings and their skin is very bumpy. At this point I feared for my life, I really thought they wanted to kill me. These two were different from other reptilians, they felt more evil and sinister. The others we fear, but I know we will be OK afterwards. With these ones I really thought I would be killed, or not going home to Amanda ever again, that I'd be taken away".

THE COTTAGE

"I don't know what happened next, because the next minute all I can remember was running for my life in a forest woodland, how I got there or escaped from those lizard men I don't know, but I was still running away from them. I knew they were behind me. I was still naked, and my feet were all scratched. I had pain in my knees trying to run. Then, in the

46

distance, I saw a few lights, but they were far away. Whilst running away from these lizard men, I started to have pains in my chest and neck. Eventually, I got to a wooden house that looked like a Swiss log cottage, and climbed up some stairs onto a porch, and banged on the doors screaming for help. A man opened the door and children were coming down the stairway at the back of the room. I ran upstairs saying "Help me, call the guards I'm from Dublin". A lady covered me in something, and some of the older children in their late teens who spoke English, told me that I was in Germany, in a town called Baden Baden. Then two tall men, like the men in black, dressed in grey uniforms came into the house. By now I was crouching down and hiding in a boy's bedroom. Then suddenly a strong light flashed in the room, which changed to a blinking light. I looked down at my body, and it looked like my body was dissolving. I was then somehow taken out of the boy's closed bedroom window and found myself on a craft, the light inside this craft was a very white, pulsating light, which made a low then high pitched noise. This light was blinding and hurting my eyes and making me feel dizzy. I asked them not to hurt me, and to bring me back. I said that I wouldn't hurt them, that I only wanted answers. I wanted to know why us? Why do we have so many different 'beings' around us, and for what purpose? They never spoke, they just stared, and their eyes were black. They were not slit like a snake or a cat, they were just all black".

CHANGING EYES!

"Then I woke up at home. Amanda stared into my face and said that my eyes looked funny and that they were changing colour, from blue to white. I also noticed that I had difficulty focusing my eyes. Amanda knew something had happened to me by looking at my face. My body was frozen cold with fright. Normally I am strong with some of the 'beings' that I've seen, even although some of them scare us. But I can control myself, but these ones were pure evil. I can't remember anything else".

"Malcolm, I know it happened, because even though my feet and body were clean, the bottom of my feet had scratches and

*bruises on them, as did my right shoulder and my face. I also
had small pine needles in between my toes! The only pine
needles around my home, are 30 minutes walk from me in St.
Annes park. The mountains are over an hour away by car!
Surely I would have been seen by numerous taxi drivers as I
live on a main road. Not only that, Raheny Road is around my
corner, where lots of folks would be coming back from the
pubs, and there are two Garda stations on each end with patrol
cars going around. Coolock Garda station is further up
Tonlegee road, and Raheny Garda station is just before the
turn into St Anne's. I did wonder if I had sleep walked and
dreamt the rest, but I remember how winded and in pain I was
as I was running. I remember seeing the lights in the distance
and the look on the couple's faces when they opened the door of
this cabin in Baden Baden and saw me, hysterical, and trying to
ask for help as 'they' were after me? Then, as I've stated, I saw
some children gathering upstairs and was told where I was.
Then I remembered other abductions or pieces of our
experiences over the years and I just knew it was real".*

(Author's Note)   Patricia mentions above, that in this dream
(or Abduction) the lady of this house told her that she was in
the town of Baden Baden. Baden Baden is a spa town in the
state of Baden-Wurttemberg and lies at the North Western
border of the Black Forest Mountain range on the river Oos. If
this was reality and not a dream, then we should ask the
question, 'why are these 'beings' dropping Patricia off in a
different country to her own? Was this a mistake, or was it
planned this way? And for what purpose? Patricia continues.

*"Furthermore, I'm sure the craft I was on, was a Reptilians
craft, similar to the other one that I found myself on with the
strange girl Julia, but this time I was absolutely terrified of
something. I don't remember what they were doing, or how I
got outside of the craft when it landed in Germany, as I say, I
only remember running through the forests down a mountain,
yet I'm crippled with osteoarthritis and I can hardly walk, let
alone run. Unless adrenaline played a huge part. Like I've
said, it was the next morning in bed as I woke up in pain, when*

48

I said to Amanda to look up this place that I was taken to last night.

NAKED FEMALE ALIEN!

"I keep seeing these strange markings in front of my eyes, like hieroglyphics but more jagged that resemble lightning flashes. But on both occasions recently both our bed covers were pulled right up to our chins, and I remember before I was taken last night, it looked like the floor was actually opening up between our beds with a whirlpool of white light and those three small beings being close, thankfully I didn't see the 'Hat Man' last night"

(Author's Note) Patricia stated to me that she had written the above on Amanda's i-Pad/Tablet as her laptop wouldn't work and failed to charge. She said that she was about to call me when she had the phone knocked out of her hand. Then she saw the 'Hat Man' go through the room while calling me, and that she was now freezing cold and shivering. She went on.

HUGE CRAFT.

"A few weeks passed when Amanda and I decided to take a stroll one night to a small park near the Capuchin Friary and Hospice near our home in Raheny. It was around 9:30pm. As we began walking through a grove of trees, Amanda got frightened, as she had seen several coloured lights in amoungst the trees. I told her that we were nearly out of the clearing, but instead of going towards where you see the lights, I said, 'Let's go this way" and we turned right into a clearing which effectively was just a huge field and walked on. In the distance there is a children's playground with a large round woven swing that we sometimes lay upon on when there is no one around at night. Just as we were halfway there, a huge craft flashed at us, and then it shone a white light down towards us. This craft was moving ever so slowly above our heads as we approached the playground. We both lay back on some swings watching this amazing large craft but then started to feel very

49

uneasy as if something bad was going to happen, yet our uneasy feelings were not associated with this craft, as we both still felt safe with a feeling of protection knowing that this craft was part of our 'Sky Family'. As we left the playground, we heard shouting from an estate nearby, we then saw a host of Garda cars and a Garda van, and what we believe were detectives in cars all screaming past us in the distance. The following day we learned that there had been a huge drugs bust as well as rival gangs all fighting one another".

"A few more days passed, and Amanda and I were out in our back garden as we regularly are, depending on the weather. We were with our friends, Margaret and Paula and we were all gazing up at the sky, when we all saw the most awe inspiring and outstandingly beautiful large spiral in the sky which was changing colours and moving around majestically. We knew that some of our other neighbours saw it, as we could hear our neighbours saying that it wasn't foggy out, so that it couldn't have been some strange fog lights, but you could hear in their voice that they were just as excited as us. We initially thought that there might be some event in town which might have been casting laser lights up into the sky, but we later found out that this was not the case. All of a sudden the spiral vanished, and in its place was a craft which flashed a white light three times and then flew slowly overhead before vanishing".

STRANGE CREATURES IN OUR BEDROOM!

"In 2020 Amanda and I were both getting into bed when we both heard a strange electrical hum which was making a buzzing and clicking sound. Suddenly, a very heavy weight fell across our feet, and when we looked down, we both saw a 'being' that we have never seen before. The utmost dread and fear came over us. This 'thing', was lying across our legs. It was pure black and looked as though it was wearing some kind of armour, it's body shape reminded us of an Armadillo but the thing was, this thing had the head of a 'Grey'! We stared at this incredible creature whilst scared out of our wits, we both saw that on this 'thing's body, on its back and sides, were some

50

swirling white blinding lights which we believe was giving out this strange noise. I threw my arm across Amanda to protect her, but In an instant we were thrown out of bed and onto the floor, onto a pile of shoes next to our built in wardrobes. And then suddenly, as if things couldn't get any stranger, a bright red light flashed through our bedroom window at which point, more of these black Demonic 'beings' all in different sizes suddenly appeared in our room. One small chubby bodied 'creature' which was pure black and about three feet tall, was trying to pull apart my legs. Another smaller thinner being, was on top of my chest, and I remember grabbing it and banging its head backwards on my wardrobe a few times. I don't think that it had a neck, but later on, Amanda said that it did. Two others thin beings like the Grey's were beside Amanda, and even although their heads were shaped like the Greys, their mouths and chins had the shape of a duck bill"!

"At this point I was trying to say the 'Our father who art in Heaven' prayer, and call upon Jesus, when all of a sudden our bedroom door flew open, and another flash of red light appeared, followed by a sinister looking seven foot 'being' who may have been even taller and who was bending down to get through our doorway. He looked like some kind of insect. He was black, and his head shape was like a Grey, but his body, arms and legs were different, and I can't recall if it had that armoured feature on it's body or not. Amanda and I started to call upon Jesus to help save us, at which point this 'being' said that 'our' Jesus holds no place here, and told me to be quiet in an angry voice. The only differences that these 'creatures' have with the Grey's, is that they have no neck. They are pure black, and their skin felt like a crocodile, very ridged. They had round eyes, and their mouths were shaped outwards like a duck bill. Their hands were like crab claws, two ridged but flat fingers. There was one in front of me and a smaller one at the back. I don't remember anything else of that night".

TINY 'BEINGS' INVADE OUR HOUSE!

"As if that wasn't bad enough. Around the end of November 2020, I awoke from my sleep due to feeling something crawling up my body and beside my arm under the sheet. At first glance, I thought they were mice, because we had field mice in our kitchen nesting in our kitchen sink cabinet. I quickly grabbed one off me, only to see a very small black 'being'. His head was similar to the Grey's, but slightly more human like in its facial expressions, only the eyes and the head shape were more alien in appearance, along with its body, which was long and slender and felt very smooth. They had hands and feet like ours. The other one of these small 'beings', had very smooth skin. I think it was female, and they both were tiny in my hand. The smooth one as I say, was with a group of others. Amanda was now awake, and we held onto each other. We were both startled and don't know how they did it, but they all just suddenly disappeared from my bed, either downwards or into the wall. I think I saw tiny white sparkles, however, Amanda can't recall seeing that. I watched as some of these 'sparkles' went through the wall behind us. Then, about a week later, I woke up to the same thing happening all over again. Amanda was fast asleep, one of these 'beings' was beside my face as I was laying on the bed on my left hand side. I grabbed it only to find slight variations to the others that I had seen. This one felt fuzzy, like a bumble bee, for as a child I had been stung by one. Only this one's expression was that it was frightened of 'me'! The others that I have seen and interacted with, seemed more relaxed. This 'being', had teeth, and it was trying to bite my finger to free itself. The only way that I can describe the teeth is to compare it to a lady shaver razor, not very sharp. And although this one was similar in appearance to the Greys, as far as I know, the Greys don't have teeth. Bill Rooke, a Facebook friend had asked me on Skype if I had noticed any wings, as it may have been a fairy, but we didn't. Maybe the wings were retracted into its back? Or maybe it had none. I remember it settled down when I said "Stop trying to bite me, I'm not going to hurt you". A few others just appeared and vanished along with this one. I should point out, that these little 'beings' were

only around 15 centimetres tall, really tiny. They also had a glow around them, as if they were self illuminating".

"As I was typing all this information on my tablet to you Malcolm, everything that I had put down about the above, started to disappear! The screen kept going black, then other strange things like the pixels would disappear. Not long after this, and over several occasions, Amanda was paralysed in bed, as was I. And only last week on two separate nights I woke up to find that Amanda was holding the hand of a small Grey. As soon as I saw this, I grabbed hold of this Grey's arm and told it in no uncertain terms to leave Amanda the f**k alone".

"Malcolm, when I have been writing things down for you, I've had my back and shoulders poked. I've had a small invisible object thrown at me, there has been loud banging on our piano which I can tell you was very dis-concerting, and we have still to endure all the encounters with the Greys, and Shadow People. We've had the dark brown, red and grey orbs floating around, followed by the all too familiar and disturbing visitations by the 'Hat Man'.

HOW COULD HE NOT GIVE ME CONFESSION?

"A few years ago I think it was either April or May of 2016 on the first Sunday after Easter and the Feast of the Divine Mercy. I went to mass, and after it was finished I sat for a while waiting to get confession. The Sacristan and two gentlemen were tidying up the Sacristy and counting the collection dues. Father Derek Lauder was sitting down now, so I knocked on the door of the Sacristy, the door was already opened and he said, "Come in Patricia, what can I do for you"? But as soon as I said that I wanted confession, his whole demeanour took on a new persona and he became very agitated and said, "No, I won't hear your confession, the time for that was before Easter Sunday". I looked in the direction of the Sacristan men, and I could see that they were clearly shocked by what Father Lauder had said but they never said anything. I immediately said to Father Lauder, "But today is the Feast of the Divine Mercy and our Lord specified that whoever shall recite the Novena and rescue confession on this Holy Day, shall

receive many graces and miracles, and at their time of death, I will stand before my father, not as a judge, but as their saviour allowing them passage into the Kingdom, free from all sin, and Jesus will guide us home".

(Author's Note)   Wikipedia tells us, and I quote.   The novena in honour of the Holy Spirit, is the oldest of all novenas, since it was first made at the direction of Our Lord Himself when he sent his apostles back to Jerusalem to await the coming of the Holy Spirit on the first Pentecost. It is still the only novena officially prescribed by the Church. Addressed to the Third Person of the Blessed Trinity, it is a powerful plea for the light and strength and love so sorely needed by every Christian. Patricia continued.

"Needless to say, Father Lauder was furious, and in a loud voice started yelling that he does not believe in the Divine Mercy, that it was a Polish Pope who canonised a Polish nun to Saint Hood, and he did not believe that the Lord gave her this Novena, let alone told her to paint his image that she had seen one day standing before her. Now I was in tears at this stage and extremely angry by his response, but I respected the church as it was a Holy dwelling, so I bit my lip but said, "In Catholicism it states that NO priest has the right to refuse hearing anyone's confession day or night when asked". At this, Father Lauder shouted out, "I have the right, as St Benedict's is my Parish church along with St Monica's in Edenmore. Now 'get out' you are no longer welcome here". At this, I felt a presence come over me that I can't explain. It was like someone was speaking through me, and calmly and slowly I said, "You, as a representative of the Lord, do not have the right to refuse those of 'HIS' flock to seek confession. And this is 'NOT' your church, it is the home and Earth dwelling of the Blessed Sacrament, and it's doors are open to all and welcomed into the house of the Lord your God". Then I about turned, and left Father Lauder speechless, along with the others, and started walking down the aisle".
"Just then, a very strange elderly man appeared before the exit doors. He had long dark grey hair with a moustache and

*beard, and was hunched over a little, and he looked as if he was
homeless. I was nearly crying at what had just gone on, and I
knew this man was looking at the tears welling up in my eyes.
He just stepped forward, and gently took my hands in his, and
said, "Pray for me". I asked him what his name was, and he
just said, "A friend", giving a faint smile. I just stared at him
in bewilderment wondering who the hell he was. I was saying
inwardly to myself, "I don't know this guy do I"? At which
point, the man gently placed one of his hands on my shoulder
and asked again, "Will you pray for me, and him" as he
pointed to Father Lauder. I turned around to light a candle at
Our Lady's statue, and as I did so, I said "Yes, I will pray for
both of you" I quickly turned around to face what appeared to
be a destitute man, but he had vanished, completely vanished. I
was stunned. I quickly opened the doors at the end of the aisle,
but he was nowhere to be seen. Now I believe that this strange
man was Jesus, who through time, has appeared to many. But
he appeared to me, as a humble, passionate homeless friend on
the Feast day, because only he knew what his Novena and Holy
picture means to me. And as I honoured him, I got the feeling
that he wanted to let me know, that both Amanda and I are
always protected, and whenever needed, we can count on him,
our Lord Jesus to be here for us. I now understand why a
priest told me 13 years ago, that both Amanda and I were
blessed".*

*"As I mentioned earlier, I am adopted, and I found my birth
mother Barbara Nicholas during my mother's illness, where I
spoke with her and found out that I am of gypsy blood. My
ancestry is Amazique, Berber tribe, and French. At least now I
know why I love the Moroccan, Arabic, and Bohemian style"!*

(Author's Note). Wikipedia tells us, and I quote:
"The traditional Berber religion, is the ancient and native set
of beliefs and deities adhered to by the Berbers (Amazique
autochthones) of North Africa. Many ancient Amazique beliefs
were developed locally, whereas others were influenced over
time through contact with other ancient Egyptian religion, or
borrowed during antiquity from the Punic religion, Judaism,
Iberian mythology, and the Hellenistic religion. The most

recent influence came from Islam and religion in pre-Islamic Arabia during the medieval period. Some of the ancient Amazique beliefs still exist today, subtly within the Amazique popular culture and tradition. Syncretic influences from the traditional Amazique religion can also be found in certain other faiths". Patricia continued.

"My brother Walter has also seen things that he can't explain. I feel it's part of me, and I do believe in past lives. I am very strong when helping others deal with evil, but scared in my home, as I fear for Amanda. We are both psychic, but will not use our gifts around others, because it make things worse for us. We attract more negative beings. We always say to them "Peace be with you, we mean you no harm".

"I mentioned earlier about our Sky Family. Well I should point out that before we even knew about Steven Greer and CE 5, we could go out in our back garden and ask our Sky Family to illuminate their craft when they are overhead as a sign that we know it's them"

(Author's Note). For those who are unaware who Steven Greer is and his CE 5 programme, he is one of the world's foremost authorities on the subject of UFOs and extraterrestrial intelligences. Steven and his followers have been initiating peaceful contact through his CE 5 protocols for a number of years in the hopes of establishing contact with Extraterrestrial beings. Over the years, he and his followers have witnessed some bizarre lights in the sky which they believe are attributed to coming forth through his protocols.) Patricia continues.

"With some of the UFO sightings that we have seen, we feel pure love and bliss, but with the others, we get a dreaded fear that will sweep over us. We are tuned to our feelings and know when 'they' are around. Back in 2009, my daughter took photographs in her bedroom and was astonished to see the image of a family which consisted of a man and woman holding a baby at her wardrobe"

(Author's Note) Sadly when I asked about what had happened to that photograph, Patricia told me that this was taken on one of Amanda's old mobile phones which got broken, and she lost the photo when she got a new replacement phone. Patricia continues.

"Several months ago, Amanda pulled over our sitting room curtains, and we saw a blue, smokey light streak across the floor. Lately we are seeing what I call 'water beings' because they resemble water shapes of small people coming from our fireplace and moving towards our television. I was in my kitchen one night, and for some reason I asked if there was anyone present to give me a sign in the name of God and all that was Holy. I then heard a flash/crack and saw over my garage, a green/rusty coloured orb floating towards my back door. I opened the door and it came inside then moved to the left of me. I closed the door and it floated beside me on the door in front of me. A crackling/sizzling noise came from it, and I was drawn to reach out and touch it, but when I went to it, it got bigger, growing almost to the size of my head. At this point I let out a loud scream, then burst into tears running down my hall for my daughter. When we came back it was gone".

"In the summer of 2010, my daughter was out with her friends, I was in the living room watching television when I heard some whispering to my left. I turned around to look, but I was paralysed with fear. My chest felt like it had enormous pressure on it, as if something was knocking the wind out of me. I just stared at a picture of Jesus that I had beside my television. My eyes were being forced closed even though I was trying to keep them open. I kept hearing this whispering then nothing. A few days after that, I saw 'The Hat Man' on our fourth stair in the hall, he then formed into smoke and drifted up to the attic".

DO YOUR WORST!

"One night in March 2015, my daughter and I were once again feeling very uneasy, we had a sense of a presence in our home, followed by a putrid smell of what I can only describe as

a mixture of fish and bleach. We had this smell many times before, but mostly in late summer and early autumn. This smell would mostly be on the landing, and our front bedroom. But this night it was everywhere. We both felt nauseous, and fearful, more so this time. It was only when my daughter Amanda said that she couldn't cope with this any more, that I flew into a huge rage with it. I said "Show yourself", and I started to provoke it, saying "Come on I'm here, why are you hiding from us, terrorizing us, yet and not showing your true self to us"? I said, "You are spirit energy, I am human with the protection of my Lord and Saviour Jesus Christ, we have been through hell all over the years, but we are still here, what can you do"! Nothing happened until we went upstairs to bed later that night. We both still sleep together, and during the night we both heard scratching and walking around in our attic, which is above our bed. Then a built in wardrobe on Amanda's side, started to rattle loudly. At this point I felt a burning feeling, very painful, on my right side above my hip. I got out of bed, put on the light and pulled my nightdress up. Amanda said there were three long scratches, from my lower ribcage to my hip but these scratches, although new, did not bleed. And it healed and vanished in around four days".

"Then there was the time that I was in bed when my daughter rushed up the stairs terrified, and told me someone was knocking on the doors that divide our front and back sitting room. Our bedroom door and living room door open by themselves from time to time (with no windows open) We hear loads of creaks and walking in the hall, stairs, and landing. Amanda took a picture of a boy/man sitting on our stool hunched over in the backroom, but the old laptop that we had stored the photograph on broke, so we don't have the picture. I told my uncle, a Franciscan Priest, in South Africa (Father Dominic Hession, now deceased) of our experiences, and he said there was a presence around us but it was not evil (but I beg to differ). We still have our house lights flickering on and off for no reason, and also our television will switch on and off, again for no reason. Then there are the footsteps we often hear. I know that houses creak now and then, and there could be faults in the electrics, but I can't explain the other goings on".

"A few years ago, 2017 to be precise, we had emerald green spirals form all over our bedroom, from the floor to the ceiling. Five red orbs have appeared in the box room, at the same time as the spirals moving frantically close together.

SLENDER AND WHITE GRAYS.

"One year, I believe it was 2019, something happened. About 10 minutes after getting into bed, I noticed a side view of a black shadowy 'Hat Man' on the wardrobe. I told Amanda to move closer, then all she remembers is seeing the shadow then it moved in a wispy fashion to the window. Whilst doing so, she had an odd sort of elevator feeling grabbing her head, and she reached out for me but couldn't talk. I tried to pull her closer to me telling him/'Hat Man' to get the f**k away from her and that I've had enough. It was then that I noticed three very small Grey 'beings' towards the end of her bed, but they weren't the usual Greys, they were more slender and glowing white, about 2 foot tall. All of a sudden, I felt something come between us, holding me down. The next thing I remember, is being dazed and seeing illuminating white light that almost hurt my eyes. I then saw a metallic table with a white surround, and seeing taller beings. Everyone was in white, it was almost like I was under water and I don't remember much after that".

CREEPY DOLLS

On April 27th 2020, Patricia sent me some further information which I found intriguing. It had to do with creepy dolls. She stated.

"Many years ago when Amanda was around 18 or 19, which would make it 2007, 2008 she had these creepy little dolls called little apple dolls. They wore white masks over their faces that resembled the Grey's, and held an apple studded with pins in their hands which came with a haunting story about how each one had died. I never liked them, and told Amanda I felt uneasy with them. With all we have experienced over the years in regards to abductions and other paranormal activity, I

59

*honestly don't know why she was attracted to them. But one night when a little dog of ours broke a bone in his foot, we carried him upstairs to bed as he slept in-between our wardrobe. We were in bed and heard footsteps scurrying back and forth under our beds, we turned on the light and Ranger was just waking up from sleeping in the same spot between the wardrobes. I turned off the light, and after a short while heard it again, only now it seemed more like footsteps. We turned on the light again, and Amanda said she thought that two or three of the dolls had moved position from where she had placed them, as they were arranged differently. One doll was even completely naked! I picked them all up, all five of them, and placed them in a garbage bag, which I then left in our back bedroom, ready to throw out the next morning. It took us a while to go back to sleep but we did. Next morning, I went into the back bedroom and was horrified to find the garbage bag opened sideways on the floor, and one doll was in the middle of the floor (The night before I had left the bag upright, tied in knot against the wall!) and her mask and clothing was removed! I cried in terror for Amanda who rushed in and just said "What the "f**k". We quickly got dressed and I dumped them in a skip behind our Tesco's, that was before I had disassembled them, breaking them up, so that no one could use them. Amanda told me afterwards, that she doesn't know herself why she wanted to collect those dolls because of how terrified and traumatized she has been over the years with our other negative visitors. I feel something played with her mind to buy them. Indeed, I bought two for her also, and don't know why! so that's the only reasonable explanation I have. But I felt uneasy about them from the start. We only had them for a few months, and nothing happened that we were aware of before that night".*

ALL THAT GLITTERS!

(Author's Note) On another e-mail, Patricia asked me if the chemical element Iridium resembles glitter. This was because she has had quite a lot of silvery glittery bits showing up on her body, these were more noticeable during the summer months.

60

Patricia further stated, that Amanda has noticed a little of this glittering effect on her body as well. She went on to state that some of her friends had noticed this, and asked her if she was out partying, and had somehow got glitter on her. The effect was also noticeable when they both washed. I then decided to have a look at what Wikipedia had to say about Iridium, it stated, and I quote.

'Iridium is a chemical element. A very hard, brittle, silvery-white transition metal of the platinum group. Iridium is considered to be the second densest metal (after osmium) with a density of $22.56g/cm3$ as defined by experimental X-ray crystallography. However, at room temperature and standard atmospheric pressure, iridium has been calculated to have a density of $22.65g/cm3$, $0.04g/cm3$ higher than osmium measured the same way. Still, the experimental X-ray crystallography value, is considered to be the most accurate, and as such iridium is considered to be the second densest element. It is the most corrosion-resistant metal, even at temperatures as high as 2000°C. Although only certain molten salts and halogens are corrosive to solid iridium, finely divided iridium dust is much more reactive and can be flammable.

(Author's Note) I asked Patricia is these white glittery spots still appeared on her body, and she replied that they did, however, these glittery spots, were now mostly appearing on Amanda's arms.

Divine Mercy Picture, flew off the wall (c) Amanda Hession

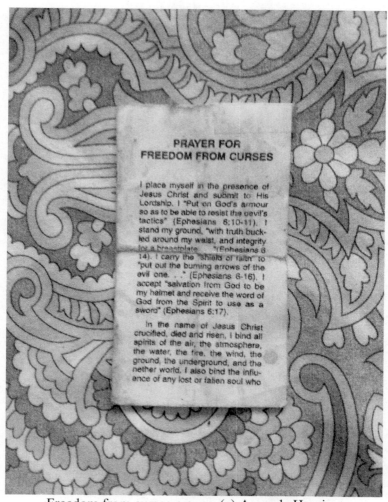

PRAYER FOR FREEDOM FROM CURSES

I place myself in the presence of Jesus Christ and submit to His Lordship. I "Put on God's armour so as to be able to resist the devil's tactics" (Ephesians 6:10-11). I stand my ground, "with truth buckled around my waist, and integrity for a breastplate . . ."(Ephesians 6 14). I carry the "shield of faith" to "put out the burning arrows of the evil one. . ." (Ephesians 6-16). I accept "salvation from God to be my helmet and receive the word of God from the Spirit to use as a sword" (Ephesians 6:17).

In the name of Jesus Christ crucified, died and risen, I bind all spirits of the air, the atmosphere, the water, the fire, the wind, the ground, the underground, and the nether world. I also bind the influence of any lost or fallen soul who

Freedom from curses prayer. (c) Amanda Hession

Holy Items (c) Amanda Hession

Holy Water (c) Amanda Hession

St Anthony's Blessing and Holy items (c) Amanda Hession

PAT, SEND YOUR VISITORS TO ME!

Now anyone that knows me, knows all to well, that I want to get to the bottom of any paranormal case like yesterday, and so I decided to ask Patricia, as she claimed to be in contact with what she calls her, 'Sky Family', to come and pay me a visit. Here is what she said to me.

"I would love for you to see them. I have called on them twice before, and they appeared to two friends of mine several years ago in an illuminating amber spherical light, like a sparkler, but they have intelligence. They were not Chinese lanterns, but very similar in appearance until they get close. They suddenly appear, and in a flash they are gone. They can appear out of thin air, float very slowly, then stop and turn and change direction. Others I would NOT wish on anyone! Thank you for investigating and believing in people like myself. I pray you too will see the wonders you seek in time. You will, and I believe there are beings around you in various forms that are closer to your heart. Feel them, smell them, Ask them to give you signs, talk in prayer with them".

(Author's Note) Well, much as I tried, I could not detect any signs of Patricia and Amanda's 'Sky Family' friends. That's not to say that they might not have been around. Maybe I am just not psychically aware enough to recognise them. Perhaps in time I will get a fright, startled by something which defies logic. I sure hope so. After I had written back to Patricia telling her that I sadly did not pick up anything, she replied with.

"Pity. I will keep asking them to appear to you. It could be in their own time, not mine. I want this so much for you. Try at will to call them towards you in thought, and prayer. They may need to use your energy. Write down any strange smells, feelings, noises, changes in yourself or home etc, that seem out of the ordinary. Or just sit quietly away from others on your own and ask 'Who is with me now'? 'Tell me your name/s'.

'Give me a sign you are here'? Take it slowly from there and use your own thoughts, words and feelings to open communication with them, but always do so, in the name of God. Even if you wish to call upon a Shadow Being or the 'Hat Man'. The 'Hat Man' feeds off fear and negative energy so take care and please stay safe".

RECURRING HEALTH PROBLEMS.

Throughout both Patricia and Amanda's life, they have been troubled by deliberating illnesses. Amanda has had recurring stomach problems. Doctors first said it was gastritis, then chronic gastritis. Gastritis is the term used for inflammation or irritation of the stomach lining. It is a fairly common condition with a range of causes which range from eating foods that you don't quite agree with, to using certain types of medicines such as painkillers. Amanda has also had pneumonia, kidney infections, bladder infections, and cystitis. In 2000, Amanda had to have her appendix removed, then, years later, Amanda had to get her gall bladder removed following cholecystitis, which developed to cholongitus. Then, after all that, they said she had acid reflux. Patricia wrote to me saying that she wouldn't be surprised if all these medical conditions might be due to her alien visitations! At one point, Amanda's doctor gave her a 50/50 change of living! Although Amanda still has health issues today, she is still very much with us".

In a further e-mail that I received from Patricia, she had this to say bout her eyesight.

"Just wanted to mention this as I'm perplexed. Around 2011 my eyesight started to deteriorate and I decided to have an eye examination with Spec Savers in the Omni retail park. After the examination, I was told that I had a cataract in my right eye along with being short sighted. Two or three years after that, I couldn't see properly out of my glasses, so, while I was in town, I had another eye examination from a different business. Super Savers Opticians in Talbot Street Dublin, and they confirmed that I had a cataract in my right eye and was short sighted in that eye as well. So I decided to change my prescription and get

a thicker lens for the right eye. A few years went by, and I went for another examination, this time back to my local Spec Savers in Donaghmede. On this occasion I found out that I was very short sighted, but had no cataract at all in my right eye? On the 15ᵗʰ of February 2021, I was sent back into hospital with what my doctor thought was a T.I.A. (a mini stroke) as I told Doctor Joanna Healy, I went blind in my left eye upon waking up for approximately one minute. I also had pain in my chest running up to my shoulder, through my right arm and then into my back and jaw.

(Author's Note) A T.I.A. refers to a Transient Ischaemic Attack, or better known as a 'mini stroke'. Wikipedia tells us, (and I quote). 'A TIA is a brief episode of neurological dysfunction caused by loss of blood flow (ischaemia) in the brain, spinal cord, or retina, without tissue death (infarction). TIAs have the same underlying mechanism as ischaemic strokes'. Patricia continues.

"The reason I went to hospital, was that I'd be waking up in the middle of the night and also on some mornings, completely blind. I'd only see colours in both my eyes. Then on other occasions, I'd see spots of blue in my left eye, followed by blackness for several seconds. That was two years ago, but a few months ago this spotty light effect, lasted for about a minute, along with severe pain in my chest running through my shoulder, arm, and back. I was taken to Beaumont hospital where I stayed for five days having numerous tests done, such as blood tests, ECG tests, echo location tests on my neck and heart. I had a full body brain scan and had both eyes tested but they couldn't find anything wrong with me. The other night Amanda saw a bright white light which almost blinded her in both eyes, but was put back to sleep! I know. I've seen this light aboard craft! I'm just wondering if this cataract was an implant? Because cataracts do not disappear on their own. This doesn't make any sense"

BLAISE OUR DOG SENSED 'SOMETHING' IN OUR ROOM.

"While I was in hospital, Amanda told me that our dog Blaise was very unsettled, this was on the 18th of July 2021. Blaise was pacing the bedroom floor while Amanda was in bed. Amanda told me that she felt very anxious and uneasy, when all of a sudden Blaise jumped up onto the bed and was looking around at something, something that only she could see. A few nights after I came home from hospital we awoke from our sleep as Blaise was pacing the room from my side of the bed. Then she went back to Amanda snarling and growling. This time I sat up with Amanda, but we did not see anything, yet we both felt terrified as Blaise continued his barking at something in the corner of my room on my side. I got up out of bed at which point Blaise charged over from the other side of the room to guard me. As she got in front of me, still barking, I climbed back into bed whereupon she jumped in between us whilst looking up and staring at the ceiling. Amanda and I started to pray for whatever this was to go away. Eventually Blaise settled down and went to sleep. However, this strange behaviour from Blaise continued for a further few nights, then it petered out and she was fine after that. On the 9th of July 2021, both Amanda and I were watching television in the evening when all of a sudden there was a huge loud crack beside Amanda on the window. We initially thought that someone had thrown a large stone at the window, but upon immediate inspection, there was no stone or any object lying around, and there was no damage to the glass, not even a scratch. Later that night we went to bed as usual. I woke up around 05:30am to go to the toilet, and when I got back into bed, Amanda told me that she felt dreaded fear, and had that crawling sensation and pressure go up her body just as she had got into bed and lain down. She said that she tried to shout out for me, but found she was paralysed and couldn't speak.

THE 'HAT MAN' RETURNS

"On the 15th of July 2021, both Amanda and I felt very uneasy and anxious all day, we didn't go to bed until well after 01:00am. As soon as we got into bed, I placed my right arm across Amanda because Amanda was terrified to move, shouting out, "He's here, he's here" I also felt 'his' presence. Anyway, I looked towards our bedroom door, and our old familiar nemesis was standing there. The "Hat Man'. I sat up in bed, and for some strange reason, I began talking to him. The thing is, I can't recall much of what I actually said to him, other than asking him to tell me who he is, and why are you always around us, and what do you want? I even asked 'him' if he wanted us to pray for him, if he wanted forgiveness from us or from God, and if we prayed for him, he could go back to God! I remember telling him that we wanted to communicate with 'him', the Greys, and others, so that we could put our minds to rest and possibly have an understanding of them, and their motives. At this point, 'he' began to move forward and stood at the foot of our bed. I told 'him' that we are fed up of being afraid, and I will not allow this dreaded fear to take hold of us any more, and either he communicates with me or not. I told 'him', that this was 'my' house, that its our home, and 'you', along with your other dark negative 'beings', are not welcome. As I finished telling 'him' off, both Amanda and I started to pray, and I called upon our Guardian Angels, Jesus, Mary, the Holy Spirit, and Almighty God and our good Sky Family to give us protection. At this point, 'he' moved over to my side of the bed near the corner where Blaise my dog had previously been barking at, and I said again that I wanted to know about 'him'. I wanted to understand 'him', and why he continued to terrorise not only us, but others as well. WHY? Why won't you say something? 'He' leaned over me and just transformed into black smoke and vanished".

SENDING OUR 'HAT MAN' TO ANOTHER PERSON

"Now I was wondering whether or not to tell you about this Malcolm, but at the end of the day, I guess I should be

completely honest about 'all things', although what I am about to tell you was maybe something that I shouldn't have done, but anyway, here we go. Many years ago, it was either 2015 or 2016, my friend, Margaret's sister Paula, who is special needs, was being used as a punch bag by Margaret's partner's brother, with whom she was in a relationship with at the time. Both Margaret, Paula, and Morris's brother, Dean, asked me if I could get rid of Morris from their home as they were all afraid of him and did not want their brother Colin knowing about what was taking place in regards to his abuse on Paula. Now I don't know what power I possessed that day, but I believe that I controlled 'HIM' through the hatred and anger that I felt towards Morris. So I called upon him, yours truly, 'him' who I fear, 'The Hat Man', saying, go to Morris and Paula's and do your worst. Get rid of that fellow in the house now. A few minutes after I said what I did, I got worried sick, and told Amanda that I think he is going to attack Colin, Margaret's brother, realising that Colin had the day off from work, and the fact that I had said 'fellow' instead of Morris. Realising this, I quickly rushed round to Margaret's and started banging hell out of the door and ringing the bell. The door was quickly answered by Colin who had a duvet wrapped around him, and said, "Come in", he looked as pale as a ghost, and immediately slumped down on the stairs. Clearly something had happened to him. I kept asking him how he was, but he was reluctant to part with any info. I kept probing him, but he kept saying that I would think he was crazy. So I told him what I had done, and who I had sent to the house, and the reason why I did so. Colin was the only one in the house at the time, as Morris, who 'was' in the house, had left in a hurry, feeling decidedly uneasy. All the others who were usually in the house, were out shopping. Eventually Colin opened up and told me that he woke up feeling a strange sensation that was creeping up his body which started to pin his body to the bed. He then experienced 'something' choking him, but he couldn't see anything in the room with him".

In a further e-mail to me, Patricia was aghast at what she had written previously. She stated.

71

"Looking over the above comments, prove that I was insane and not in my right mind acting out like I did, but I hate woman beaters and criminals. Anyway I got rid of all negative beings including my friends. I cannot fight others battles for them. And they say they can forgive him because it was the drink and smoking weed that made him the way he is. I can only keep them in my prayers. Sorry to have bothered you with this. I guess all this upset and agro brings on the shadows as they feed of this rage and fear. I don't have all the answers, or know why I sent this 'being' to them, I guess they have to fight their own demons, so to speak. Still trying to figure out what I am a part of, but I do know for a fact that my daughter and I are different from most folk".

THE 'HAT MAN' IS SENT OFF AGAIN!

During one of the continuing discussions that I had with Patricia over the years, I asked her if she could send me her 'Hat Man'. Even with all the research and evidence that I have accumulated over the years, I still want that 'in your face' evidence. I know that after all my research I should accept what I've learned, and take it on face value, but there is still that part of me that wants more, that wants to see, and feel the paranormal right in front of my face. Yes, I have indeed experienced the paranormal throughout my life, (most of which has been written up in my previous books, *'Paranormal Case Files of Great Britain' (Volumes 1, 2 and 3)* available on Amazon. But I guess I am one of those guys who wants to test the water more than the norm, to put myself into situations that should provide the paranormal thrill that I am looking for. I think ultimately, I want to capture on film, an actual ghost, that after all the necessary tests have been done on it, which can rule out fakery (of which I'd never do in a million years) people would say, *"Well, there is no denying that Malcolm has indeed captured something".* But there lies the rub, even with that tangible evidence, there would be those that would still dispute this, so we are back to square one. Evidence is in the eye of the beholder, but those other eyes from other people who were not there at the time, will always have a hard time in accepting it.

72

Anyway, getting back to me asking Patricia to send me her 'Hat Man'. She stated that if I saw him, I'd regret it, as 'he' is not a pretty sight to see. I should also point out here, that Patricia then wrote off to a friend of hers, one David Baxter, who, as it turned out, *she also sent the 'Hat Man' too.* This was because David had angered Patricia by making accusations about her daughter and herself being involved in Black Magic and stating that they were Satanists. These accusations were of course untrue, and were in all probability, borne out of learning that both Patricia and Amanda had weird 'stuff' going on in their house. Here is what she wrote to him.

"Was chatting to a very dear friend on Facebook, who is in fact a researcher/investigator on UFOs and Paranormal activity, Malcolm Robinson is his name, and he would like to experience the 'Hat Man' that I sent you in anger. Did the 'Hat Man' ever come back to you? or was it just that one time? I prayed, begged, and asked for the 'Hat Man'/shadow being to go to Malcolm, but he didn't. Do you think I have to be angry in order to send him"?

David Baxter replied.
"Yeah the last time I kind of pissed you off, that was when a weird feeling kind of came over me and I felt uneasy in bed. So I think it only happens when you're angry or pissed off at someone, would I be right"?

Patricia replied.
"I do believe so. What exactly happened? so I can tell Malcolm. How did the 'Hat Man' make you feel"?

To which David Baxter replied.
"I just felt that someone was looking at me in the corner of the room I would gasp out loud a good few times. It's bizarre. But I hope it won't happen again".

SEEKING HELP FROM OTHER QUARTERS.

It was clear to me, that both Patricia and Amanda needed help, and needed help fast. Most of the correspondence that I had with Patricia, was when I was living in Hastings on the English South Coast, (I now live in Sauchie, Central Scotland) and Patricia was many miles away in Ireland. There had to be someone closer to her that could lend a hand and hopefully alleviate the situation. Well she managed to get in touch with an Irish Demonologist named Richard Bailey asking for his help. But sadly it bore no fruit, as Richard did not believe Patricia, he thought she was joking! Nevertheless, Patricia gave Richard my phone number where I awaited his call, but he never rang, and I couldn't get through to him. However, Patricia persevered and managed to get Richard to open up and talk further with her. Here is what Patricia had to say about that conversation.

"I was on Skype last night with demonologist Richard and his associate Freddy. They said after speaking to us, that even though I had these 'beings' with me since birth, that some of these 'beings' may have picked up on energy from an uncle of mine who was a Roman Catholic exorcist, as he gave us presents, etc. They told me to get rid of everything associated with my uncle. (Father Dominic Hession, now deceased) I also remember a time when I was 15 years old, just after my dad had died. I made friends with a new girl in school and I told her that my mom and I were not getting along, because she blamed me for my dad's death. This was because I had told my mom about a premonition that I had a few days before he died of a massive heart attack. This girl invited me to her home, and she had an Ouija board. I did not partake, but sat there as she asked questions regarding my dad, I can't recall much of what happened. I also told Richard about the time that my friend Beverley was using the Ouija board when I was in her house. Anyway, this Demonologist Richard, said that these 'beings', Demons that Beverley had, could now be with me, although I did not participate in those seances, I was just there. I told Richard and Freddy That I was adopted, and found my brother

74

a few years back, and he too saw beings, including the 'Hat Man'. I believe these beings are in our bloodline, and ancestry"

"Richard told me to get rid of any clutter, anything that is no use to us in our home. We are now stripping the walls and we will start to paint our home in brighter colours. Richard said that he hoped to visit us again in the future, but sadly he never did. Freddy told Amanda to stand directly under our attic doorway and using telepathy, to face her fears, and tell the 'Hat Man' to leave her and me alone, and get out of our home. Well, we tried that, and all hell broke loose in our attic. We were freezing, trembling. The attic was creaking above us. Richard told us to get him, 'Hat Man' and 'them' out of our minds, and not to think or remember them in any way. We have tried all this over the years, then when everything we think returns to peace and normality, they come back again and hit us full force. But we will try all the help and advice we are given"

I also put Patricia onto another Irish Paranormal group, but sadly they didn't get back to her. Now I have often said to many people, especially any audience that I give a lecture to, that I am 'not' an expert in these matters, I have never claimed to be. It saddens me that some of the media that I have worked with over the years, claim that I am! I guess that's the down side of working with the media. Every UFO and paranormal researcher has their own take on the paranormal. Some are serious, whilst others come away with the most ridiculous statements which can often upset the witness. Indeed, Patricia told me about what Richard and Freddy had said to her, which she was none too pleased about. Here is what Patricia relayed to me in an e-mail.

"I have been very upset that no one got in touch with me about my situation. Richard and Freddy only chatted once on Skype, but he had me weary, as Richard asked me who my God was, and about my faith and beliefs. He also told me not to have anything more to do with my religion because it was them who brought on the demons to me in the first place! I was ready for a huge fight with him, as many cultures around the

75

world speak of demons since time began, yet I kept my mouth shut, so as not to bring on any more negativity. Richard was supposed to get in touch with a UFO group in the U.K. that he said would help me, but no news yet. Anyway we had two more experiences since last week, and one of our dogs barks three times every hour, from 11:00pm till 6:00am since we moved our beds into the box room. While we are re-decorating our bedroom, he never barked like that before, and we used to be extremely terrified of the box room, as many strange occurrences happened in there. Yet I have my relics, holy pictures, holy water etc. in that room while we are in there. Other than that, all is well, for now at least".

"Also Richard is convinced that Amanda and I are involved with Ouija boards! I told him no way on God's Earth would we entertain that. I did go to a home several years ago to try and help a lady that I used to pal about with to help her remove evil from her home, as she and her children were involved in all sorts of occult activity. Richard said because I went there, they could have latched onto me and came home with us. I told him I had many 'beings' long before I knew the lady of that house. Don't forget, these beings were around me since I was a baby from what my parents told me of the many strange occurrences that surrounded me back then. I know we are not harmed by them, yet the experiences cause Amanda and I mental distress, but I have lived half my life with them. I only wish they would converse with us and tell us exactly what and why they are with us. They do speak sometimes, yet most of what they say is blocked out, and we get only pieces here and there which we try to put together".

Whilst I was in communication with Patricia and Amanda, I was always looking to put other Irish UFO and Paranormal groups onto her. Sadly there were not a great deal of them, but those that I did find, I did pass on Patricia's details to. As we can see from above, only a few replied. When I mentioned this to her, she stated.

"Not to worry. Maybe all the 'beings' we have here are too much for some to comprehend. Or because we have a mixture.

Those who specialise in one field, may not wish to deal with some of what we've got so to speak! Spirits, orbs, light beings are one thing, but Demons, 'Hat Man', Shadow Beings and then the extraterrestrial's, are all a bit much for some to take on. Thanks for all your help and concern for us, I will try my best to search here in Ireland with Tim Kelly ghost hunters who work on paranormal activity surrounding Dublin hotspots, such as Wicklow jail, the Dublin and Wicklow mountains, and see if he can assist or know someone who can. I may have to call in a Jesuit priest, yet I fear some of them, even though it is my religion. I do not trust many of them or the Vatican. For my own safety and Amanda's, I think they might lock us up in an institution if you know what I mean. I have heard that being done to people in the past in some extreme cases. Even though our experiences are the truth, they would have us assessed by specialists and tell us we have psychosis".

(Author's Note). Patricia told me that Tim Kelly the paranormal researcher never got back to her.

SINISTER DARK FORCES

"I feel there is a sinister dark force at play here dwelling on keeping myself and my daughter housebound, as Amanda does not go out due to being in pain, and although she changed her diet, no dairy, wheat, eggs, citrus, spice, she still has toilet problems from extreme constipation some days, to severe diarrhoea on others. She can not go out to work or attend a course in college. And our electricity still plays up now and then. Over the years we have experienced lights flickering on and off in our house. Our television would turn on, then change channels by itself. We would see just a white noise on the screen, and a strange voice would come through the screen which we couldn't make out. The light on our porch would switch itself on and off, with nobody near it. And when I would go to turn the lights in our hallway off, they would come back on again, all very frustrating. Our home phone would crackle and strange noises would come through it. We would also hear clicking on the phone and strange voices that we couldn't make

out.   Then the phone would suddenly go dead.   Light bulbs would constantly pop in the living room and we were forever replacing them.   Some of the above have been seen and witnessed by our next door neighbours".

It was clear to see in all the e-mail communications between Patricia and I, that there was still quite a lot going on. My main concern for both her and her daughter, were their ongoing health problems. In an e-mail to me, Patricia stated.

"Amanda says she gets severe pain in chest behind the sternum. It feels like stabbing pins and needles like a cactus poking her on the inside.   She gets this several times a month, and it takes her breath away for a few minutes. Our doctor still does not know what is causing this.   They just keep prescribing medication. I often wonder if our health problems are a result of our UFO abductions. It's all very strange because my knee was on the mend until I contacted the Irish demonologist lad, after that, all hell broke loose".

A BREAK IN COMMUNICATION

Then suddenly, I stopped hearing from Patricia, it was a good while before I heard from her again. When she did reply she stated.

"A long hello to you Malcolm, and many apologies for my disappearance from Facebook for several months. I felt myself at a loss, drained, fatigued, and broken down, due to the fact that I spoke to the Archbishop of Dublin's secretary for advice and immediate help in dealing with all the negative aspects of the supernatural that we are experiencing, but got NO HELP from our church authorities. They received all the information from my childhood experiences and that of my daughters. This included information on 'beings,' 'spirits', 'orbs', 'light anomalies', 'The Hat Man', 'Shadow People'. Also 'the greys', 'reptilians', and the old man and woman we've seen, and the long haired girl that moved very fast. Then there is the 'water blob beings', and pure 'demonic entities', and not forgetting

78

our abductions, to the point that we are starting to recall some experiences, and craft, and seeing many 'beings' while we are fully awake, even in the daytime. A cat that is not ours, appears and vanishes before us. And a larger than usual raven sits outside our bedroom window. I understand all of these sightings and experiences will seem untrue to many, as I told all this to many paranormal groups when I was asking for help. Even the groups you posted to me last year Malcolm, well I think that 'they' think we are lying, that is why I always said I am willing to do a polygraph and/or hypnosis test, whatever it takes. But I was raised a Roman Catholic, practised my faith, and was blanked by my Archbishop. A Jesuit priest helped us, but we still get abducted, and have negative beings around, not as much these days, but they still come. Doctors and specialists have done numerous tests on Amanda, and found her intestines are not absorbing the fluid intake from her food. They will not perform surgery at present to give her a stomach bag, so Amanda says she has no life. My nerves are gone. I wanted us to visit all of you guys at the conference last year, but was afraid because I believe our home phone was tapped"

It was clear to see, that Patricia would go to any ends to try and get help for both her and her daughter. Indeed, she even approached Casement Aerodrome, also know as, Baldonnel Aerodrome in regards to her UFO sightings. Here is what she said to me.

"I have made several calls to Baldonnel Military base over the years to state what we have seen over and around our home. I was asked to come out to the base to be shown around and talk about my experiences, but was told to tell no other people, as it must remain private? So my mind was going haywire. My daughter and I are depressed and anxious. I must try to be strong for us both. I have gone back to work in my local community centre as a youth worker in the evenings and Amanda is on a disability allowance"

Incidentally, for the benefit of the reader, Casement Aerodrome or otherwise known as Baldonnel Aerodrome, is a Military airbase which sits to the Southwest of Dublin in

Ireland. It can be found situated off the main N7 road and is the headquarters and sole airfield of the Irish Air Corps. The base is also used for other government purposes. Baldonnel Aerodrome is also the home of the Garda Air Support Unit. Patricia went on.

"I just don't know. Even with our Holy water, Holy pictures, Holy medals, and crucifix in our bedroom, 'they' still come. We pray and bless ourselves every morning and night with Holy water, all to no avail. And we have different 'beings'. Each of which, are worse than the first ones. I ask God to keep them away, because we have other beings we do not fear. I don't know if the good ones are angels, or just other alien beings protecting or observing us. Its all too much right now. Anyway thanks for being here and listening to a woman who feels crazy".

PICKING UP ENERGIES

Patricia is a woman who I would say is clearly psychic, and picks up on energies not just around her, but also others as well. Not only that, she can pick up bad vibrations from various locations. In my opinion, her being psychic, is sadly allowing her to pick up on all these disturbing things that have been happening in her life. In a further e-mail, she talks about picking up and tuning into distressing feelings of long ago. She states.

"We went on a Dublin ghost bus tour with friends two nights ago, and one of the sights was St. Kevins church in Dublin. A ruin that has a lot of bad negative energy, which includes a Satanic black mass and rituals. There was also a monk who was tortured by having iron type boots placed up to his waist, and then filled with oil. He was then hung up over a fire. White witches were also persecuted there too. I felt disoriented and dizzy there, and the guide was concerned asking me if I was alright, he knew something had happened to me. Yesterday I was in a rage for no apparent reason, and my daughter was the same. We both wanted to hurt and injure each other, this lasted

for several hours, until she saw two very large black orbs. I saw them as Shadow Beings, but more evil. Amanda got Holy water and threw it over me, and then I got up and used white sage to cleanse my home. I thought we were OK. Until now. I feel there are more folks out there that are under attack and are afraid to come forward for various reasons, mostly of being deemed ridiculous, or crazy, and outright lier's etc. Although as you yourself Malcolm and others have stated, there could be other explanations for what is happening, but only when they are ruled out, can one truly believe the other!

WE SEEM TO HAVE THE LOT!

In a further e-mail to me, Patricia began to detail even more of her thoughts and feeling regarding the experiences that she and her daughter Amanda have had to endure. She stated.

"We used to blame the Grey's and Shadow People and also the 'Hat Man' for some disturbances, but deep within, we knew that we also had a poltergeist, and yet we were more terrified of the 'Hat Man'. I read in your book of the hooded monk, well we also had hooded shadow beings. I wonder if a slight change in the frequency of their energy could account for the poltergeist activity? Are they the same entity or individual? Yet to us the 'Hat Man' is Demonic, as is the poltergeist. It's the way we have a dreaded built in fear when they are making their presence known. We have smelt smoke, burnt toast, and a putrid fishy bleachy smell in our home, but I used to put the sweet floral scent smell down to angelical, holy, protective, as we had no feeling of fear associated with that smell. But I do know these entities are very intelligent and cunning. We also heard each of us call the other, but when one of us said "What do you want"?, the other would say, "I never called you". The few passages that I've read so far in one of your books Malcolm, have put a lot of truth into perspective for me"

"I was scratched down my back and neck, and pushed. And both Amanda and I were thrown out of bed, but we only told my uncle Father Dominic Hession, now deceased about it. I only spoke about some of our accounts of the Shadow People and

'Hat Men', including the Grey's, reptilians, the orbs, and tall white beings, and lately we have had the darkest black ones that resemble the Grey's in body, but their eyes are different, and they also threw us out of our bed a few months ago. We both landed on Amanda's pile of shoes beside the wardrobe. When I sought help before I asked you, many told me that I was imagining all of the beings, as most people only have encountered one or two. We seem to have the lot! I used to make a joke about them by saying 'family reunion' eh. I am open to you using our real names for your book, as I am sick of hiding the truth as it may help others come forward. I am still happy to undergo any polygraphs tests, or to go under hypnosis with anyone you wish to be present, to tell you and them, my truth. I feel some or all of the Grey's, work under Lucifer. I may be wrong but it's niggling at me. Also The 'Hat Man' may, or may not, be Lucifer, or something similar. As angels have hierarchies, I believe so do they, ie the Grey's, Reptilians, then Lucifer's dark angels, then him"

(Author's Note)   What proved equalling interesting to me, was when I learned about Patricia's home phone being tapped, and also that she had seen a lot of Military activity near her home.   She and Amanda have also had to put up with their phones and i-Pads/Tablets continually malfunctioning, as we will see from her next post to me. She stated.

PHONE TAPPED!

"I have been watched by military helicopters and had Range Rover type vans which have been parked in the estate across my road, directly in front view of my house. I'm pretty sure that these are not owned by the folks that live there. I believe my phone was tapped, as it only crackles when I'm chatting to someone about my abductions and encounters. Sometimes it cuts off, and when I call the phone people out, they haven't a clue, as they tell me there is nothing wrong with my phone or phone line. Not only that, my laptop and also my daughter's laptop and tablets, have been hacked into regularly, so much so, that Amanda has had to keep changing her passwords".

"Malcolm It does seem very bizarre when I read back upon what I've written. Especially the black beings description. I tried to draw all our beings that I've seen over my lifetime but I'm unable to, yet their image is very clear in my mind. Yet I can draw and stencil everything else! Other folk have left remarkable sketches of the Grey's and Reptilians. But the water blobs and the black ones I have not come across anyone else having encountered yet. Although on a series about the paranormal on television, there was a very small transparent being near a small pond that resembled one, but we never saw it's arms or legs, just the shape of its head and torso. Yet it moves upon the floor. Very strange and totally unbelievable. Amanda just told me the small black being I flung against the wardrobe had a long skinny neck. The others did not".

These events are still occurring to Patricia and her daughter Amanda, indeed in August 2021 Patricia e-mailed me to tell me that the 'Hat Man' had come back a couple of weeks ago where she confronted him as 'he' stood in the doorway. Upon speaking to 'him' in a one way conversation, 'he' moved forward and stood at the end of her bed for a good while before vanishing. Patricia has always got her camera at the ready, but she stated that she just can't get any photos of 'him' as he comes and goes. Patricia stated that Amanda had 'something' pulling on her arm while in bed the previous week, but she didn't remember anything else. She went on to say that there were still lots of coloured orbs in her home nearly every night. Surprisingly, both Patricia and Amanda haven't seen much of their Sky Family craft in the sky, but she did put it down to the sky being heavily overcast with constant rain.

VIDEO OF ORBS.

In August 2021, Patricia sent me a video of some beautiful blue orbs that she had captured with her phone, (a Cubot Levona smart phone). I must admit, I have always been very sceptical of orb photographs and videos. I've said for years that for me, most of these orbs are just dust particles caught in the flash of the camera, either in dusty uncarpeted corridors, or in homes with fibrous carpets, of which, when walking along the carpet, one's feet displaces up into the air, some of these fibres, which are then captured by the flash of the camera. Orbs can also be moisture in the air, again captured by the flash of the camera. Admittedly, there are some orbs which 'seem' to defy logic, and perform manoeuvres that 'seem' to be intelligent. I've viewed lots of videos of orbs over the years, only a few have impressed me. Some have featured a few blue orbs flitting about, so when Patricia sent me her video, I must say I was impressed. Patricia's videos showed lots of white orbs, but the video that impressed me the most, showed quite a number of beautiful 'blue coloured orbs'. They were large and small, and just either suddenly appeared, or zoomed into shot extremely fast. And when she asked them to appear, 'they did', on cue. Some would say coincidence, others would not. Another impressive aspect on Patricia's video, was when she was sitting in a chair in her back room filming all these beautiful blue orbs, a strange tubular 'thing' appeared from just below her chin. (She was pointing the camera down her body at this point). This tubular 'thing', seemed to form up of a number of circular orbs all joined together to form this one long tube! It weaved its way to the left and to the right, then just dissipated. I must admit, I've not seem this type of effect before, so that kind of threw me! Patricia also took a video with her phone outside in her back garden. That particular video only offered up a few white orbs, and what have been described as Rods. For those not acquainted with the Rod phenomena, (also known as 'skyfish', 'air rods' and 'solar entities') These are elongated streaks of light which caused a big stir a few years ago, brought to the public's attention by the late American researcher Jose Escamilla who felt that these 'light beings' were some sort of new alien creature. This he promoted in his lectures after initially filming them back on March 19th 1994 at Roswell New Mexico as he attempted to film a UFO.

MEETING JOSE ESCAMILLA

On the 4th and 5th of December 1999, I had the opportunity to meet up with Jose Escamilla, when I gave a lecture at the

LAPIS UFO conference which was held at the Lowther Pavilion theatre in the lovely sea side town of Lytham St Anne's near Blackpool in Lancashire England. This event was held by the lovely Jean and Sam Wright. The title of this conference was, *'UFOs Nuts & Bolts or Flesh & Blood?'* Now there's a title! Speakers lined up were, Michael Lindemann, who was giving two talks, one on the recently released MJ12 documents, and the other was on the scenarios of E.T. contact. The ever present and well dressed (the Man In Black!) Nick Redfern (now living in the USA) was there to talk about the FBI Files and Cosmic Crashes, both titles of his successful books. George Wingfield was present to talk about black triangles, Lionel Fanthorpe unfortunately couldn't attend and speak, but pilot Graham Sheppard was there to talk about pilots who had witnessed UFOs. Graham also gave a cracking account of his own UFO sighting. Anyway, the point I am making here is, that Jose gave a lecture about the Rod Phenomenon. He captured the large audiences attention, as he danced about the stage, all excited, as he showed the audience on a large screen, all these rod like photographs that he had taken. Indeed, Jose even gave me a baseball cap with a stitched drawing of a rod on it. In the bar, back at the hotel where most of the speakers and delegates were staying, was a piano, nothing strange about that, except that during the course of the evening after the day's conference, the bouncy tones of the Beatles hit Lady Madonna began to be belted out. As a big Beatles fan myself, I turned around to see who was producing this fine, excellent tune, and was amazed to see that it was Jose Escamilla. Suddenly Jose was surrounded by UFOlogists each adding their own dulcet tones to the singing and playing. I decided to leave a full table of my fellow UFOlogists and friends, and with glass in hand, proceeded in the direction of this happy bunch of soulful songsters. With a slight cough to clear my throat, my own dulcet tones were added to the mish mash of voices that were gleefully singing to this wonderful tune. It didn't stop there. More Beatles songs followed, we had Hey Jude, Get Back, Martha My Dear (about Paul's McCartney's sheep dog) and a whole host of not only Beatles hits, but other hits as well. Jose seemed to know every tune that had ever been written. So I jokingly asked him if he knew that old Bolivian folk song from the 1920's entitled 'The Fields Are Dry', and with a wry smile he said, *"You sing it, and I'll play it"*. Great memories. Jose, you will be sadly missed.

SO WHAT ARE THESE RODS?

As the years rolled by though, and further research was undertaken by others, it was ascertained that these rods were nothing more than an optical illusion, caused by the fast motion trails of various winged insects as they sped fast across the viewer with his camera. They sure caused a stir in the field of the paranormal, and they are of course still being photographed today. Patricia as I have mentioned, captured one of these 'rods' herself, but I made it known to her what these were. In the next chapter we will look at Patricia's friends who have backed up, both her and her daughter, by also experiencing what they have seen.

CHAPTER THREE

Friends confirm the bizarre events

Needless to say, you can't write a book about a families paranormal events without getting some back up to their story. People would quite rightly ask, *"Well what about friends and family, did they witness the events"?* It's true to say that thankfully there were a number of other witnesses to these strange events that both Patricia and her daughter Amanda had to endure. However, whilst compiling this book, I found out that not all witnesses to what had gone on, wanted to speak to me. That I can understand, as this is common from people who witness UFOs, ghosts, poltergeists, lake monsters and such like. People's integrity can be questioned. People are fearful that they will not be believed, or worse still, poked fun at. I've always said that for every one person who comes forward to report a ghost, there could be many others who might have seen that same ghost, but refuse to come forward for fear of ridicule. Its a sad indictment of society, and it takes guts for people who are prepared to come forward and relate their stories of the paranormal. Nobody would willingly want to go through what Patricia and Amanda had to go through, but they were prepared to come forward and share their story, so that others who were going through similar events, would know that they didn't stand alone. As stated at the beginning of this book, I have had to use pseudonyms for people throughout this book which I never like doing, but I have to respect the wishes of those who do not want to be identified. I would say to the reader that using false names in no way diminishes the fact of the honesty and integrity of the accounts given, and those that were happy to share them with me. So, without any further adieu, let us turn to the first of those individuals who have come forward and backed up Patricia and Amanda's experiences. We firstly hear from Patricia's next door neighbour Paul Sullivan. This is what he had to say.

PAUL SULLIVAN   (Next door neighbour to Patricia)

Hi Malcolm,
"Good to hear from you, and thanks for reaching out regarding Patricia and Amanda. My mother, father, sister and myself, have been next door neighbours to Norah (Patricia's mother) and Patricia, since approximately 1985. Norah and my mother were very close friends and never far apart from each other. Norah was an extremely religious person, and truthfully the kindest soul I've ever encountered in my life. Both of our families live in either half of a semi-detached house".

"The paranormal or strange incidences that my parents mentioned to me are few but noteworthy, considering both my mother and father are/were sceptics. When Norah was near the end of her life, Patricia set up her bed in the downstairs sitting room. On the night of Norah's passing of a brain tumour, (September 26th, 2007) Patricia called my mother and father in to sit next to the bed and comfort Norah, say prayers etc. Norah passed away, and my parents didn't mention anything about what they had seen/felt out of fear and shock, and probably so as not to frighten my sister and me. Throughout the following weeks, through drips and drabs, I did manage to get some information out of my mother and father".

"My mother felt the presence of a 'being' behind her as she held Norah's hand on her death bed. A cold chill, and the smell of flowers enveloped her. She was terrified, but Patricia told her it was a good spirit and was there to protect everybody. The lights in the room started to flicker and dim, and went on and off at different intervals throughout the night and day. My mother said she saw 'things' she could not explain (I took this as figures/shapes/lights or maybe orbs but that's just me speculating. I'm not sure if my father was present at this time, but this is what he told me he experienced in the room after Norah has passed".

"Immediately after Norah's passing, the TV turned on, which had not been on in days. The channels started to change and through the white noise on the channels, a strange sound was coming through. To note, no actual TV channels came on just white noise. The way in which the TV turned on was also unusual. It made a popping noise and the screen opened from a small dot in the middle of the screen, then enlarged to fit the full screen, like it was being zoomed into, or like an old TV would from the 60s/70s. My father jumped up and ran out of the room"!

"I wish I had some more information for you Malcolm, but this is the only paranormal experiences my parents had. On a side note, I mentioned to Patricia years ago, about the time my sister ran into my bedroom one morning, completely terrified, saying there was a man at the end of her bed. She had just awoken, so it could've been sleep paralysis, but Patricia is convinced it is the same man that visits them. My sister shares a wall with Patricia's house bedroom".

"Also, Patricia told me when my mother passed away, she was in our sitting room where the wake was. She went over to my mother's coffin and said "Sleep in heavenly peace." That night when she was home, a musical ornament started to play the notes in 'Silent Night' for 'sleep in heavenly peace'. I should point out that this ornament was not programmed to play 'Silent Night' it played a different tune!".

"As I mentioned earlier Malcolm, my father is a sceptic. I have no problem with you including this information in your book but if you could please use a pseudonym I would appreciate it as I wouldn't want to upset him".

Kind Regards Paul.

Now, we have read throughout the book about Patricia's friend Beverley. It would seem that in some strange way, Beverley was like a paranormal battery of sorts when it came to strange things occurring. Nine times out of ten, when the two of them were together, strange things started to happen. It was apparent that I had to get Beverley's side of things. Patricia's friendship with Beverley was not always on a good footing. There would be rifts in their friendship, and they would not

89

speak to one another for weeks on end, but at the end of the day, they always got together, and when they did, there was always something happening which not only frightened them both, but made them realise that maybe they should do something about it. As we have learned, Patricia sought help from the Church and Paranormal Investigators, none of which really alleviated the situation. And whilst I, the author of this book, could only suggest people for her to turn to to seek guidance and help, it sadly wasn't always forthcoming.

Let us now turn to Patricia's friend Beverley, and learn how she endured these paranormal occurrences, not only within her own family home, but at Patricia and Amanda's home as well.

BEVERLEY BOOKS

Hi Malcolm,
"All I can tell you is that I have been seeing spirits since I was three years of age which my mom told me about. I can remember when I was around five or six years old, I saw a man walk through a door, and I told my grand mother about it. Also when I was eight, I saw a ship/UFO in the sky, dad got me to draw it, then made fun of me and stopped me from telling people what I was seeing. I knew I was different. It was not until I was in my adult years that I fully understood why. I now know that I am an empath. I know things, and sometimes feel things. The reason Patricia and I fall out all the time, was that I envied her knowledge, like a child, I wanted to know everything, I'm still learning. I have given readings to people and found out that I was correct in what I was telling them. I should point out that both my aunt and uncle are gifted as well, I only found this out a while ago. My uncle said that 'my gift' keeps changing. I'm being tested. I also believe aliens exist and I have had encounters with them".
"I must say, that I'm no good at remembering dates, funny that, probably why I failed history in school. As I've told you, I've seen things from a young age. When we moved into the house that I'm in now with my two daughters, I soon noticed

that we were not alone, we moved in 20 years ago (2001) One day the girls were playing with their dolls house in their bedroom up stairs, whilst I was sweeping the stairs with a dust pan and brush. I suddenly felt someone tugging at my trouser leg. I shouted to my daughters to stop tugging at me that I would soon be done, at which point both my daughters walked out to the landing and said, "Mom we're in here playing". Then I noticed that my trouser leg material was sticking out in mid air, it was as if a small child still had hold of me. Then, whoever was holding my trouser leg and pulling it out into mid air, let go, and the material fell back in place. I looked up at my daughters who didn't seem to see what I saw so I said nothing more. The following day, the dolls pram seemed to rock back and forth as if someone was putting the doll to sleep. For a while the house was quiet. Then when I was pregnant with my son, my eldest came down the stairs and said that she could see an old man standing on the landing with a rope around his neck. After that, she slept in beside her sister for a while".

"I first met Patricia when my partner back then had bumped into her in the street. Patricia was taking Amanda around the doors sponsoring. I got on really well with Patricia at a time when my then partner and I were having problems. Then there were the times when my children would climb into my bed with me saying that they could see a girl sitting on the end of their own bed. My ex had to sleep on the sofa when we were going through a tough patch, and on one occasion when he turned out the light, I could see red eyes looking at him. He thought I was nuts because I could see red eyes looking at him and he could not. Our relationship didn't last, and we split up soon afterwards".

"After my ex and I split up, Patricia kept in touch, she would come over to my house for dinner the odd Sunday, and in return, we would go to her house. We talked at length about what was going on in both our homes as we more or less had the same strange things occurring. We started doing seances."

(Author's Note. Patricia would dispute this, that said, Patricia did partake in one séance which in point of fact was more of an Ouija board session as we have read earlier, but in the main, Patricia wanted nothing to do with seances or the Ouija board. Beverley continues.

"We would use a glass and all sit around the table, the glass did move. We had a piece of paper with the word 'YES' at one end of the table, and at the other end we had the word 'NO'. We got a few answers. Then suddenly Amanda and I noticed a door appear on the wall. I rushed and got my cam corder to film it, at which point I could see lots of people coming through the wall. There were old men who were showing their hate at me as they glared in my direction. I saw all this, yet all the others only saw smoke! I quickly played back the footage but sadly there was nothing there. Later that night, Trisha chased a blue ball of light out of my home after we had heard a voice say, "No" One time when Steven was a little older, he and I were in Patricia's house where Patricia asked him to look at a family album and point out her dad. Steven had never seen a photograph of Patricia's dad. Anyway, he pointed to a man, and said, "This man was a drunk all the time, and this other man is your dad". On another occasion, Steven was playing piano in the back room in Patricia's house, when Patricia recognised the tune he was playing, she asked me if Steven was starting lessons, I said no, he has never had any lessons, at which point Patricia asked my son Steven how he knew how to play that tune. He quite causally said that the lady up stairs who said hello to me, showed me what to press. Back at my house things got a little worse. My eldest daughter decided that she wanted to stay with my parents for a sleep over so it was just myself, my second eldest, and Steven. They were all in bed fast asleep when I was awoken by the bedroom door opening by itself. Now I knew that I had locked up before I had gone to bed. Then I felt a heavy weight on my tummy, like someone was sitting on me. Then, in a creepy voice, I heard someone making fun off my faith and of the Holy pictures that I had on the walls. At this point I started to say the Lords Prayer, no sooner had I done so, than this creepy voice started to try and make me forget the words, but I carried on. Then it said it would wake the kids. I felt my arm go free and I put it over both my kids to protect them. I then shouted at the voice who was laughing, and said you are not welcome here. I then asked for help from God, and also our Holy Mary, and Arch Angel Michael. I asked this presence to 'GO' and said you have no right to be here, at which point the bedroom door slammed shut which woke the kids. My kids asked, "What was that noise"? To which I said that I must have banged it too hard on my way back from the toilet, and asked them to get back to sleep. Thankfully, since that night I've not had an experience like it".

ORBS

"Many a time when I've been in Patricia's house I've seen orbs. I watched once, as a load of pink ones came down the stairs and stopped in front of me. Funny enough, I had to use the loo after it. On another occasion I saw a yellowish non human figure standing behind Patricia, it was taller then her. She didn't believe me, and said that I was making it up. Then on another occasion my son Steven said from our house, that there is something going on in Patricia's house, so we rang her, and Patricia asked my son what he saw, whereupon Steven said that he had seen a green ball in her kitchen which started off small then become bigger".

(Author's Note) Although we have read earlier in the book about Patricia witnessing this green orb, I e-mailed her again to confirm this. Patricia replied.

"Hi Malcolm. Yes! That was the large green orb that appeared around Halloween after my mom passed that I wrote about. It appeared near my glass back door. It was small, the size of a tennis ball at first, then it grew to the size of my head. It made a sizzling, crackling sound when I tried to touch it and grew much larger as if to warn me not to interfere with its structure, energy. I don't believe it would harm me but I screamed for Amanda, when she came it vanished"

Let us now continue with Beverley's testimony. In a further e-mail to the author she stated.

"Believe it or not, I soon got used to all the strange things going on in my home, and after a while they became second nature. On one occasion, my son Steven was playing up stairs and I heard him talking to someone, I didn't think much of it at the time and continued with my chores. The reason I didn't take too much notice of it, was because when I was young, I used to make up voices for my Cindy dolls. When Steven came down for lunch I asked him how his game was going. He looked fed up, so I asked him what was wrong, and his reply stunned me, for he said, "I can't play the same way he can". I replied, "The way who can"? To which he said, "He can move the teddy's without using his hands. He can make them go around and around". Needless to say, I was a bit shocked at this, and asked him what does this man look like. He quickly said that he was my size and wore dark glasses. I asked him if he was still up the stairs, but he said he didn't know. It's very hard when your son describes something that I saw myself before I was pregnant with him".

"I should also tell you this, as this is really bizarre. My ex and I were trying to make a baby but were not having much luck. I had the feeling that I was pregnant, but I wanted to wait a while before doing the test. My period was late, three weeks late in fact. But I seem to recall being in a sort of hospital. The floor was very white, as were the walls. It was very hard to see where the floor ended and wall started. The beds seemed more like the hospital trolleys with out the side on. I noticed that I had an army coloured green curtain around my bed. I tried to get up and go for a walk, but a nurse wearing a green uniform, a mask and head gear with black glasses, told me I was to stay still, and that it wouldn't be long now. I then remember hearing somebody scream, as if they were in a lot of pain. At this point, I put my hands on my tummy, and to my utter shock, I looked and felt very pregnant. I screamed out in shock, then I remember that my trolley bed was rolled into another room where a lot

of nurses were standing around me. They opened my legs, and put their hands down below, then I felt something being pulled from me. I then heard someone say, "boy" then "girl" then "babies". When I looked at these 'nurses' around my bed, they looked human but yet did not! Someone then said to me that your babies can't go with you, they wont live if they do. I didn't even get to hold them. Then the room seemed to spin and I found myself back in my own bed and my nose was bleeding. The following day I went to my local G.P. who told me that I had a miscarriage. I cried for a few days after hearing that. Then, two months later I was expecting Steven".

"I told Tim Richards who is a friend of Patricia and I, about the time when I was doing the ironing, and I saw a tall grey 'being' stood in front of me. This grey said nothing and I was not frightened, it all seemed normal to me, then it left. I have seen their ships for years. I saw a silver object float down the end of my street, if anything it looked like the shape of long table. with table cloth. The object. Or whatever it was, was all silver, and it had symbols on one side of it. It was as if it was for my eyes only, as no one seemed to notice it. It was huge. I've also seen lights in the sky that covered the sky for miles. Over the years, my relationship with Patricia, has at times, been fractured, but we always get back as friends. Being an empath, I somehow know before it happens that our friendship would come to an end. I have had to make some big changes in my life, meaning I cant have negative people around me which were my family. In doing so I found myself, and met my new partner. I used to think I was a weirdo because I saw and knew things that others did not. I also have no time for religion that pushes its faith on you".

"Oh, and there was the time when I was in Patricia's house and my mobile phone rang, it was my sons school, they said that he had fainted in the school yard and that they were taking him to hospital. Patricia and I got there before the school people did, and we found my son staring into space, and then he suddenly fell to the floor. I asked my son what he remembered, and he said that he saw a ship/UFO land in the grass, and that a door opened, and 'they' wanted him to go with them. Thankfully he said no, and he was given the all clear by the hospital. I asked him about this episode a few hours later, and surprisingly he couldn't remember a thing! And to this day he has forgotten everything, he cannot remember that event at all".

"I also see lot's of little golden orbs flying around my house, even my son is starting to see them. There are what I call Shadow People that I've seen, they move so fast that you have to ask yourself, "was that real"? I've also heard voices answer me before my son does. We are being listened to all the time. I know that there are other beings here in my home, I can sense them. Some of them want your book to go ahead, as they want to be known, however, not all of them are friendly. I have been sleep walking a lot lately, last time I found my self standing at the front door with my head touching it and my hand was on the handle".

"Another strange thing was, I gave Margaret, a friend of Paula and mine's a reading. During the reading, we could both hear the sound of water pouring onto the floor. When we looked down at our feet, sure enough, there was a very small amount of water on the floor between Margaret and her partner Dez. None of them had a glass or a drink at the table. Anyway, I cleaned it up, and threw out the cloth. As I've said, I have given people readings who have told me that I have been correct. It takes a while for their loved ones to leave my home. I have got used to them popping in. Some are nasty, and they bring with them a horrible smell, but the more I ignore them they tend not to stay. Honestly Malcolm, I am telling you the truth always. As an empath, I believe that if I lied it will fall back on me, which means that I would be sent all manner of horrors".

I WAS ATTACKED!

On Sunday the 15th of August 2021, I received a disturbing e-mail from Beverley Brooks, Patricia's 'on and off friend', She stated.

"Malcolm I was attacked last night by five 'beings' who held me down. One was sat on my stomach whilst the others were trying to do something to my tummy. My son and partner heard me scream in pain and they said that my legs and arms were spread open but they managed to get me on my side. I was shaking with fright. They said that after this event I had walked in my sleep. I don't remember any of it. I fear that they might come back. My partner said that he had never seen anything like it before. My son said that I was screaming at them to stop as they were hurting me. Then I calmed down and saw a blue light. I also heard drums and wolves howling, and I shouted out the word, reptilian. Has this happened to anyone else?

I responded to Beverley by asking if her partner and son could physically see what she was being pinned down on the bed with, to which she replied that they couldn't, but they could see the fear and alarm that she was in. She also said that her partner and son suddenly experienced a cold wind which entered and pervaded the whole room whilst she was being pinned to the bed. This instantaneous 'wind' then dissipated.

Let us now in the next chapter, show you the reader, that Patricia and Amanda do not stand alone with their own sightings of the 'Hat Man' and Shadow People. We now take a look at other individuals who present their own personal experiences with the 'Hat Man' and Shadow People. This clearly shows, that the Hession family do not stand alone, and that this is an enigma, that we all should be concerned with.

CHAPTER FOUR

'Hat Man' Experiences As Told By Others

I felt that I couldn't write a book such as this without drawing comparisons to other world wide 'Hat Man' and Shadow People accounts. This needed to be done, to show you the reader, how massive this world wide enigma really is. There is no two ways about it, we really are dealing with something that has been part and parcel of humankind since probably man first walked on this Earth. There will of course be those people who will poo poo all these stories, saying that they are nothing more than wild exaggerations, sleep deprivation or some kind of global psychosis, which, when all is said and done, is in itself quite something. So let us delve into some of these world wide accounts which I hope will show you the reader, that Patricia Hession and her daughter Amanda, did not stand alone in the weird world that belongs to the 'Hat Man' and 'Shadow People'.

Graeme Kelly   *'Shadow People'.*

Out first case comes from Graeme Kelly from Edinburgh Scotland, and whilst the following incidents do not contain any 'Hat Man' stories, I felt that I should present it here to illustrate that it's not just the 'Hat Man' and 'Shadow People' that have been seen in bedrooms, other 'entities' have been seen as well. This is what he had this to say.

"For a while there I could see people when I closed my eyes to sleep at night. Out of the darkness, figures would manifest and seem to be aware that I could see them. Some were groups

of people walking outside in wooded areas, they would actually stop and wave when they saw me. Others, once they manifest, would make strange movements over and over. I've had an old guy with a chequered shirt, I've seen women in old fashioned frocks, a woman with a purple dress, demon like faces with red eyes. All this would be 'before' I actually fell asleep, I would roll over and tell Sara what I seen. I wasn't scared, more excited to see what happened the next time. Was it my brain acting up from over working, or something more! It happened for around two months, then slowly stopped. Some say it's like seeing people long gone at times when they were alive, or seeing into another void/dimension. Occasionally it was like thousands of stars passing me as though travelling through space before a strange coloured vortex like shape appeared in the centre! Not something I would share with anyone, but interesting enough I thought I would tell you as you investigate such things"

Graeme Kelly.

Our next example comes from a fellow paranormal researcher from Kingston Upon Hull in England, Mike Covell. Mike is not only an accomplished author of a number of books on the paranormal, but he also provides guided tours of his home town. Mike lives with his wife, three children, and what he describes as, a neurotic cat, and a budgie called 'Jack'. Here is what Mike had to tell me.

Mike Covell. *'Slenderman Tale'!*

"I've told this story a few times and feature it in my walking tours. For years I had access to the basement levels that stand beneath Hull's Royal Station Hotel and the adjacent Paragon Railway Station. We ran a series of nights in there with a handful of investigators, carrying out investigations, taking measurements, and documenting it for the future. As we held these events, we found that more and more people wanted to join, and at one point a lad from the staff wanted to join us. He worked on the reception in the hotel, and admitted that he had never actually been down into the closed off sections of the

hotel. We were only too happy to take him down. At the start of the entry, there is a long corridor that stretches some distance, and has about 70 % light coverage, with the end of the corridor being in complete darkness. As you approach the end, walking towards the darkness, we often had people remark that it was pretty scary and they wanted to turn back. On turning back, and seeing the light, most people relaxed a little. As such we used to say to people "If you get scared, look back towards the light." Many did this to prepare themselves"

"One night this receptionist lad came with us, he was stocky, pretty sceptical, and only came down for a look, by his own admission he wasn't really interested in the stories about ghosts. As we walked towards the darkness he was near the back, and he said that it looked scary, so we shouted back to him to look back to the light. He did this, then had the loudest freak out in a confined space that I have ever heard. He lost it completely. I ran back to him and he was shaking, crying, and wailing. I asked what the issue was. He said that he had seen 'The Slenderman'. I pointed out that the Slenderman was a fictional character, and he eventually stated that it was a tall man in black clothing, head to toe, wearing a black hat, but he could not see his face. I accompanied him upstairs, he ordered a stiff drink from the bar, ordered a taxi, and handed his notice and his keys in that night. The hotel is Victorian, and was the place to be seen in the Victorian period with Royalty passing through on several occasions, as well as a number of 'Jack the Ripper' suspects, 'Yorkshire Ripper' detectives, and Laurel and Hardy staying over. I remarked that he probably saw a Victorian gentleman, dressed in his evening attire, but as you can imagine, word spread, and a week later people were asking where they could see 'The Slenderman,' and 'Hat Man'

Regards, Mike Covell

Steven Jaws Stewart *'My Partner Saw 'Hat Man'*

Our next story comes from a gentleman from Livingston West Lothian Scotland, who, although not seeing 'Hat Man' himself, was quick to tell me about his partner seeing him. This all came about after I had shared a drawing of 'Hat Man' that I had placed on my Facebook page. Here is what he had to tell me.

"My partner used to see 'him' all the time, growing up in a house in Linlithgow. She would wake up and see 'him' and then try to tell her sister who she shared a room with, but her sister couldn't see him. She has also seen 'him' a few times in the flat we shared, but thankfully has never seen him in our current house in Livingston. This became an on going joke in their family till I listened to a podcast on the 'Hat Man' and showed her the drawing of 'Hat Man' that you had on your Facebook page Malcolm. She said, 'That's him'. She said he felt familiar and was never scared of him, indeed she felt at ease with him. And since we have had our daughter, she hasn't seen 'him'.

Steven Jaws Stewart

Michael Rutherford   *'Hat Man' Stood In My Doorway'*

Next up, is Englishman Michael Rutherford, from Barking in Essex, who not only has witnessed UFOs, but has had a few experiences with the 'Hat Man' as we shall see.

Hi Malcolm.

"Yes I have seen 'them' in my old flat where we lived in Barking Essex. I saw them quite often out of the corner of my eye, and the odd shadow with the hat shape, like the picture you placed on your Facebook page. Once when I was sitting at my PC, a shadowy 'Hat Man' stood in the door way. I looked in his direction and he just disappeared quick. I got a slight look at his eyes, and they were red. It is scary, but I do get used to them. It's like they are watching me. I even saw two of them together".

Michael Rutherford

Russell Brinegar *'Hat Men' UFOs And The Paranormal'*

We cross the pond to the United States of America for this next account. Not only has this gentleman seen the dreaded 'Hat Man', but has also had a few UFO experiences as well.

1961

"I was 6 years old, and remember very few glimpses into my early childhood prior to this one particular evening. My mother, father, and I, lived in a trailer in Merritt Island, Florida. My bedroom was located in a small room between the bathroom and the living room against the far wall. My mother had just turned out the bathroom light, and came over to tuck me in. She left toward the living room, and turned out the light in my room as she left and closed the door. I laid in my bed on my back, my eyes adjusting to the darkness. When they adjusted, I was lying there awake. I saw in my peripheral vision to the right, two figures that caused me to move my head to the right. The two figures were humanoid, one appeared to be male, possibly wearing a fedora type hat (I'm not actually sure about this detail), this could be confabulation based on 'Hat Man' stories over the years, but I distinctly felt it was a male figure. The other figure appeared to be female. They both slowly glided over to me and were standing by my bedside. I was merely curious to keep looking at them, but I felt no fear. They both bent over at the waist as if attending to me in some way. This lasted for a few seconds, then they returned to an upright position and just stood there. Then they faced each other for a few moments, and then simply vanished. This memory has stuck with me all these years (I'm 65 now), and over the years I have wondered if it was just an after effect of the light my mother turned off, like a 'photo flash' effect, but this was the routine she did every night as I was put to bed, and this memory is the only time this occurred. I never knew really how to categorize this memory, so I just filed it away in my mind as an 'unknown'"

1966

"I was now 11 years old, and living in Titusville, Florida. I remember walking down the driveway on a sunny day to get the mail. I looked up, and there were 5 to 6 disks hovering in the air, bronze to pewter in colour, and they were so still it looked like a painting above me in the sky. When I saw them, my reaction was to drop to my knees and cry, because I was afraid that they were going to leave without me, and I wanted to 'go home' with them. I do not know the actual nature of this memory, whether it was in 3D, a day dream, a nocturnal dream, or whatever, but the memory and scene has been stored in my memory as significant, just like the two 'Shadow People,' all of these years ago".

1978

"I was 23 years old, and this entire year I had weekly, sometimes bi-weekly episodes of 'sleep paralysis,' in which I would wake up in the morning, conscious, but unable to move my body. I did not like the way this felt, it was as if someone was wringing my brain our like a dish rag, and it took every once of concentration I could muster to 'break free' from the grip of this, and restore movement to my body".

1979

"I was now 24 years old, and was driving with a lady friend at night from Indianapolis, Indiana, to Bloomington, Indiana, which is only a 1 hour drive. I was driving back around 1:30am in a green Toyota Tercel. The next thing I remember, is pulling up into my lady friend's driveway to her apartment at daybreak, around 05:30-6am. I was very tired, and asked if I could sleep on her couch. That's all I remember. Margaret and I parted company after this, and we did not reconnect until 2012 on Facebook, 33 years later. She was quite surprised that I did not remember what actually happened. I was stunned as she told me that on that particular night, she had seen a luminous orb that was getting bigger, and she thought it was chasing the car. She says she yelled at me to go faster. When she said this on the phone, I did recall her saying that, and putting the pedal to the metal with a frantic passenger. She said when we got to her place in the morning, the white dress she had worn for my sales convention in Indianapolis was covered in mud, and that she

103

felt 'violated.' While I was sleeping all day on her couch, she burned the white dress outside on the bar b que grill, as she wanted to get rid of it. After we parted and lost contact, she said she contacted abduction researcher Budd Hopkins, and he said she needed to find me for a hypnotic regression, but she never could find me, as I had moved out of town shortly after that. I have no memory of owning a green Toyota Tercel, but a family member confirmed that I did, in fact, own such a car. This is unusual for me as I remember all of my cars Ive ever owned except that one".

(Author's Note) Russell went on to tell me in his e-mail that he was a "Physicalist," and was in philosophical orientation until August 18th, 2009. Wikipedia tells us that Physicalism (quote) "Is the metaphysical thesis that 'everything' is physical, that there is 'nothing over and above' the physical, or that everything supervenes on the physical. Physicalism is a form of ontological monism a 'one substance' view of the nature of reality as opposed to a 'two-substance' (dualism) or 'many-substance' (pluralism) view. Both the definition of 'physical' and the meaning of physicalism have been debated. (unquote) Russell continued.

"I had a near fatal heart attack and experienced a NDE (Near Death Experience) in which I encountered several ethereal beings in my yard where I was mowing my grass. When this happened, I had a 'transcended' version of myself. I immersed myself into paranormal research after this experience, made the connection between my NDE and alien abductions as a contact modality, and published my book in 2016, 'Overlords of the Singularity: The Manipulation of Humankind by Hidden UFO Intelligence's and the Quest for Transcendence'. I now consider myself "Idealist" in philosophical orientation, and believe consciousness is the ontological primitive.
Russell Brinegar.

Staying in America, Chehalis in Washington State to be precise, a good Facebook friend of mine, Cindy Dolowy had this to say about her 'Dark Entity' experiences.

Cindy Dolowy.   *'The Dark Shadow On The Ceiling'*

"Never had a 'Hat Man' sighting thank goodness! But I have had some dark entity experiences. The non-scary one was multiple, I've had too many to count. I've had sightings of a black shadow cat. I saw her for several years, usually running along a wall and darting around the corner to another room. I would see her every day, sometimes several times a day, but it eventually became lesser and lesser then stopped altogether. The other dark entity was definitely ominous. A pulsating dark 'being' up in the corner of my ceiling, a big mostly shapeless 'blob' but it did have a face of sorts, and you could tell it was focused or had consciousness. It would pulse and grow to envelop half the room aiming it's face at me and then recede and eventually disappear. Once it happened in a tent while camping. Ugh! Haven't seen it in nearly 20 years now thank heavens! I had two 'things' in my bedroom when I was tiny too! Had to be 3 years of age or younger, as I was moved to a bigger room at age 3. But there were two things in there. It came from the ceiling where there was a collection of cracks. I named that the Dishwatie. It was a greyish cloudy entity that would seep out the cracks and hover, slowly undulating and watching me. Then eventually retreat back through the cracks. The other came from the iron heater grate on my floor who I named the Snakebug. It would just poke it's snake-like head through the grate and look around, then look at me, it was never threatening. The Dishwatie was the more benevolent of the two, it scared me. My whole family knew about the Dishwatie and the Snakebug as I talked about them a lot and so did they. But I don't believe that my family actually took me seriously".

"As an adult in my mid to late 30's, there was the black growing evil blob thing in my bedroom. It wasn't mist or smoke. It was more like a very dark 3 dimensional shadow. But it moved and grew and undulated and pulsed. It also either

caused me to have sleep paralysis, or I simply was too scared to move or yell out. It was memorizing to watch, but so evil looking. I could not see through the evil black thing. It actually would wake me up. I heard a low machine like humming sound that would pulse along to the beat as the thing pulsed and grew. And it would grow to engulf half my room or more before receding and disappearing back into the corner that it came from where the noise would fade away when the thing retreated back into the corner. So bizarre but it was a part of my life for years. Frightful.

Cindy Dolowy

We now come back to the United Kingdom where fellow researcher and friend Brian P. James from Didcot in Oxfordshire had this to say about his 'Shadow Entities' that he has had the misfortune to witness throughout his life.

Brian P. James. *'The Dark Angel Shadows'*

"I had become aware of various shadow entities from the early 1990s; however, there was something of an 'evolution' of either the entities, or my perceptions. It was in May 2000 that I saw my first clear shadow humanoid observing me from the low cliffs, when I was on the beach at Hopton in Suffolk (coincidentally where the Michael Line passes from the land into the sea, and where other local researchers had MIB experiences). I then occasionally was aware of these shadow humanoids, usually motionless and apparently watching me. Sometimes they moved across my field of view by moving, I mean drifting across, no indication of any perambulation with their legs. It was in February 2001 when the first of the winged shadow entities appeared (what I have termed a 'Darkangel'), and this was the first occasion on which a blurring of my perception of time occurred. I was at my computer around 8:00pm when to my left peripheral vision, this winged shadow appeared, and I was left with the clear feeling it was watching me. I was brought out of this encounter by the phone ringing, and immediately thought 'who is calling me at midnight!' (there may have been an expletive in that thought!) The call was from

Gloria Dixon (this was the time of my active involvement in BUFORA, The British UFO Research Association), and Gloria noted that I seemed to be somewhat vague, and I explained what had just occurred. The call ended fairly quickly, and it was only then that I glanced at my watch, it was now 8:45pm, which didn't make sense either way, as I hadn't been speaking with Gloria for 45 minutes. My initial thought was that this might have even been a Mothman type entity, but in all of my shadow entity experiences, I have never seen them as having eyes, let alone the vivid red eyes associated with so many Mothman encounters. I have since been aware of these Darkangels sporadically down the years, almost always when indoors somewhere, and I always have this perception of being watched. I guess I could even term them 'Watchers'. I never sense any malevolence, despite what others interpret from Shadow entities. The major difference between this Darkangel and the other Shadow entities of various forms, is that while other Shadow entities always feel like they have been 'passing through' my reality zone, the Darkangel is always motionless, and apparently observing/watching. I am left with a definite sense of curiosity by both parties to the encounter as we observed each other".

"The other curious element has been the frequent blurring of my perception of time, most often I feel hours have passed rather than minutes or perhaps seconds, and just occasionally the inverse, where during what I thought has been a fleeting encounter, several tens of minutes have in fact elapsed. I do not get these temporal misperceptions with the other shadow entities, only these Darkangels. As with all such paranormal/supernatural encounters, there is no obvious trigger my side to initiate the encounter, it really is random and unpredictable. So efforts in the early days of setting up cameras on time-lapse or in video mode proved fruitless in capturing anything. So as usual, its a personal anecdotal encounter, and where I can't offer or provide no tangible evidence or proof. For those interested in Sci-Fi, I was more than a little taken aback when I saw the trailers for series two of Star Trek Discovery, that aired in 2019, as it featured a Red Angel, which looked remarkably like the Darkangels of my encounters. In the

series their Red Angel was a time travel suit created in an alternative universe, I wonder"

Brian P. James

Staying in the United Kingdom, we travel to Hounslow West London for our next bizarre account. An account of which this witness will never ever forget. This account was initially featured in my *'Paranormal Case Files of Great Britain (Volume 2)'* available on Amazon, but I felt it pertinent to reproduce it here, in light of the subject nature of this book. Here, in part, is this incredible story.

Kathy Baker.   *'UFO'S, Night Terrors And More'.*

Dear Malcolm,

"I understand that your time is precious and perhaps thousands of emails are sent to you regarding such issues, but I would like to discuss my experiences with you. These are the two most distinct occurrences, and without making this reply to you too long, I shall now briefly recount some of what I have experienced since I was 5 or 6 years of age. These are things that I would never have dreamed of relating to anyone else, and which I have hardly ever spoken about for fear of ridicule, or fear of them continuing to happen. These experiences were not pleasant. I first started having sleepwalking problems and night-terrors as a small child. I would often be found by my parents downstairs or in another room, screaming or just silent. This happened in clusters of nights at a time, and then would abate and stop for a while. Some of the nightmares I would remember seemed to be run of the mill. Others though were much more physical in nature, in terms of me experiencing sleep paralysis, out of body experiences etc. I would often 'fly' as if having been lifted out of my bed and down the hall and stairs and sometimes into the garden. It seemed crazy and disturbing to me at the time, but also very apparent and easy, unless I fought it. I remember my sister who shared a room actually waking up and asking me where I was

*going, before she shut her eyes and went back to sleep! These
flying experiences were always coupled with a sense that
something was coming into the house downstairs. I referred to
it as the Witch, because I can still see now in my mind's eye that
it was like a person, but not a person. It had a white face and a
black hat on, and big black eyes wearing a black robe/coat. It
definitely seemed menacing, although it did try to placate me. I
used to feel a sense of desperation and anger that it felt it could
enter my house and come anywhere near me. Accompanying
the figure more often than not, were what I referred to as the
'wolves', they were shorter and unemotional, they were grey
and used to prod me and lift me, and do what the taller figure
said to them. I would sometimes see a very bright light outside
my window before these night-terror sessions, and at first used
to think it was so pretty that it must be from heaven (!) but I
soon learned to dread it and not trust the light. I would also
sometimes see a 'pot' on my windowsill, which always
contained some little items such as a pin and dice. I remember
asking my mum the next morning where the pot was, but she
always said that there was never a pot, as if it didn't exist.
When I saw this pot at night, I would sometimes open it and the
pin would prick my finger. Then the figure would come quicker,
so I learnt not to open the pot! It all came to a head when I
woke with a terrible nosebleed one morning and was taken to
hospital, because it just would not stop. I ended up having my
nose cauterised, and staying in hospital for a blood transfusion.
As I grew up, the clear image of the figure subsided and was
replaced less often with a shadowy figure that sometimes I
would wake to see on my bed, holding me down in bed, or at the
foot of my bed, or in the corner of the room. With this I
experienced sleep paralysis, and dreaded going to sleep
sometimes for the sheer fear of it happening. When I moved
from the house in Hounslow as an adult to a different house the
next year, I had one particularly awful session of sleep
paralysis, where I had felt drowsy and sleepy, and so had
started a nap in the day. I was clearly aware that someone had
entered the house and was in my room holding me down with
clear malicious intent. I could not get up and open my eyes, and
it only stopped when I heard my housemate actually come in*

and call if anyone was home. Again this happened last year when I had fallen asleep in my living room on the sofa in the afternoon. Again I became aware of a specific pressure on my shoulders, and realised something was holding me down. I got an awful feeling of dread as if they were about to hurt me, so I fought and fought to open my eyes, and remember feeling angry and shocked. I was trying to scream but I couldn't but eventually I did, as I sat up hearing my voice. Whatever 'it' was, had sped off."

"I have glanced at the clock when I feel these experiences are about to occur, and awaken to find that the time is exactly the same. It is also always the same number, as in; 1:11, 2:22, 3:33. It really freaks me out, but I never used to like to ponder on it at all. I now regularly can only fall asleep with the light on. It's dimmed but always on. I feel that electricity somehow interferes with this happening, which could just be wishful thinking, but it makes me feel better somewhat. Very occasionally I have woken with scratches and wounds to my body and blood on my pillow".

"After I saw a UFO in 1996, I suddenly became really environmentally conscious, although I never realised this fully until years later. Another incident when I was older, happened about eight years ago, and again happened in the afternoon. I was lying on my bed and felt a glowing ball of energy enter my stomach area. I had never experienced anything like this before. After this I became more spiritual as a person. I once saw a black square shape appear and grow on my bedroom wall at night, this terrified me, and I resolved never to fear it, but to wish fervently that it would never return. It's as if I do not want to 'tune in' to a certain frequency or these things are more likely to happen. They can happen when I am relaxed, so I try to actively relax but maintain a more feeling of control when I do. I have often felt pregnant, but have not been, and have an awful feeling of being cheated, or as if something has been taken from me, hen the feeling subsides".

Sincerely, Kathy Baker.

OK, one of the most disturbing ghostly paranormal stories that I featured in my book, *'Paranormal Case Files of Great Britain (Volume 2)'* also available on Amazon, was the horrible and disturbing events that one Sharon Cooper from a town in England had to endure *(Sharon asked me not to disclose the town in the book)* Like Patricia and Amanda, Sharon really went through the mill with a whole host of bizarre and disturbing events. This was one of those cases where the spirit (or Demon), took things a whole lot further as we will soon see. If it was a disturbing case for Sharon, the poor recipient of what was going on, then hearing her account was quite distressing for me, and made me feel quite uneasy. I felt it best to reprint 'just some' of the horrible events that she has had to endure, as again they are illustrative of some of what Patricia and Amanda have gone through and are still going through.

Blaise Patricia's dog who protected her and Amanda from the Hat Man. (c) Amanda Hession

Saint Faustina. Suddenly appeared on Patricia's television
holding this book.

St Benedict's Church where Patricia was refused confession

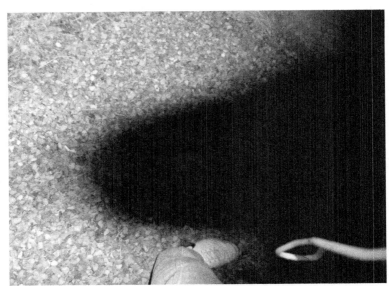

The Shadow Person captured by Bill Rooke. September 2009
(c) Bill Rooke

Where 'Slenderman' was seen. The Mike Covell story (c) Mike
Covell

Two white Orbs on cupboard door. (c) Patricia Hession.

Sharon Cooper. 'I'm The Most Haunted Woman In England!'

"I believe I could be the most haunted person living in England. At the moment. I have been haunted now for over 30 years. I feel it is time to come forward, I feel ready now. I have experienced everything from Incubus attacks Shadow People, ghosts and out of body experiences and much more. I don't mind being visited by ghosts, but I draw a line now to them attacking me. 2010 was my worst year ever. I was being attacked on a regular basis. The problem I have got, is that these ghosts visit me and follow me everywhere. I started noticing my life was different to everyone else when I was two years of age. I have sought help from my doctor and I was sectioned for 6 weeks, they were suggesting that I may be suffering from sleep paralysis or psychosis, but they couldn't find anything wrong with me. My case is very unique and rare as I can hear and see ghosts. I have been raped and dragged off my bed. I have been scratched and punched and I hate it. I want it all to stop. The ghost that I hate the most, is the one that looks something like a monk or a grim-reaper. My partner does not believe in any of it, and because he works away a lot, he is never around to witness it. He does ask where I get the bruises from on my legs. I was dragged off my bed with by partner in bed next to me, and my partner shouted for me to get back to sleep. I have lived with this for years now and I am scared for my children. My daughter told me she saw a small boy in my bathroom and in her bedroom she said he had yellow eyes".

"I saw a message on my bathroom wall with the words saying, "I will accept a child, a next of kin". My daughter said this ghostly boy strokes her arm and watches her. I told her to keep him off her bed and not to be his friend. These ghosts follow me. I previously lived in another town, that is where the monk grim-reaper ghost found me. I now live in another town. Now I don't mind the normal human ghosts, they smile at me and stare at me. It's the demons and bad ghosts that I want rid of. I have been seeking help now for over 2 years and nobody seems to be interested in my case".

116

"I found out that my gran was also visited by ghosts over 60 years ago. Her son Barry kept seeing a UFO on the field outside his house. He told my mother he saw a man in a UFO and the man was calling him. When my gran was a teenager, she saw a monk like figure that followed her for years. My gran would see and hear her son Barry in her home, he would kick the foot of the stairs to say he was home 'after' he had 'died', this continued for years. When I was one year old, I was being visited by an old woman ghost, she would talk to me. She was very nice to me, she always appeared dark, like she was wearing black clothes with a hooded robe over her head. I could never see her face. When I was 3, my parents split up, and my mother took me to live with my gran. My gran moved back to another town when my grandfather died. When I was seven, my mother moved to another town. I could hear a baby crying through the wall, this happened every night when I went to bed I reported it to my mother but she dismissed it as being a cat outside. My twin sister and older sister never heard it, which I found strange. On one occasion, I woke and opened my bedroom curtains to find a monkey like creature in ice on my bedroom window. My twin also saw this. I destroyed it because I did not want my mother to see it because it was quite scary looking. I did not want my twin scared she was screaming when she saw it. It was spiky and small like a baby it had no eyes, and it looked like it was running, it was weird. When I broke it, it melted onto my older sister's bed that was under the window"

"That night my older sister said she could feel spiders running all over her body, she was screaming and very upset. My twin reported seeing her toys at the bottom of her bed moving like someone was playing with them. My mother reported seeing a man in her bedroom with red eyes, she called him moth man. I was in bed one night and I felt someone sit at the foot of my bed. I heard a voice saying "Hello Sharon". I recognised her voice it was the old lady who would visit me when I was small and lived at Wolverhampton, she had found me. When I was nine I had the flu, and I died in my bed, at

117

which point I saw a girl in my hall, she held my hand, and was very nice to me. We would float down the stairs together, it felt great. She was a stranger, but I felt I knew her. She had long hair and was wearing a long nightdress. She wanted to take me away from my family, but I refused to go with her, she was not happy. I wanted my twin to have a go of floating down the stairs, but the girl did not want me to go into my bedroom. I ran into my bedroom and saw someone in my bed, when I looked closer I realised it was my body! The girl insisted I went with her, but I got scared, and managed to get back into my body, it took me a couple of attempts and I was sucked into my body, the pain was really bad. When I was with the girl, my pain went away. My twin said I had stopped breathing and my lips were blue and my eyes were rolled back. She said she was trying to wake me up for a long time. She said she was going to tell my mother that I was dead. My ghost friend in the hall was gone, and my twin said nobody was in our hall. For months the ghost of the old woman visited me she would watch over me as I slept".

"We all saw shadows of people at night moving around in our house. My mother got upset with it all so we moved house. We moved to another town. When I was twelve, I got a paper round job with my twin sister, everything was going fine until it was my turn to post a newspaper near the house where we used to live. I felt ill, and I noticed a man standing next to me, his eyes was glowing red, he was very tall and thin, his face was grey, and he was wearing a black hooded robe but I could see his face. He made me feel very weak. My twin was standing behind a tree with a trolley with newspapers in it. I walked away from the man and I felt a lot better, I told my twin not to look back and just to run home. I looked back and I saw the man watching us, he felt evil. We ran home where I told our mum that I saw a man in fancy dress. That night I went to bed, and I could hear heavy breathing in my bedroom I thought it was my neighbour snoring, so I turned off my light and got into bed, but I felt I was not alone. I felt the same evil feeling come to me. I felt ill and very weak. I could hear the breathing getting louder. I lay there feeling scared and I was just about to

118

get up to put my light on when I saw the same man in the robe in my bedroom, he had a smaller man with him, they were both watching me as if they were curious of me. I closed my eyes, I felt very weak, and I felt like I was in a trance like state. I wanted to scream for my mother but I was so scared, nothing came out my mouth".

"The tall one was leaning over my bed, he had red eyes and he was evil looking. The small man was like a very old man/goblin. He kept putting his face next to my face. He was very cold they both smelt horrible. I noticed the small one had breathing problems, like he had very bad asthma, he was horrible. The smell was so bad that I held my breath and closed my eyes, and I was praying that they would leave me alone and go away. I heard footsteps walking around my bed going towards my window. I opened my eyes and the small man came over to me and he was licking my face, it was disgusting. I continued pretending to be asleep and they both walked towards my window and walked through my wall. I could still hear the heavy breathing and footsteps and I felt very weak, so I lay in bed trying to figure out what had just happened to me. When I felt better, I got up and put my light on. I couldn't say anything to my family as I feared they would think that I had dreamt it all up or was making it all up. I saw my gran and asked her if she believed in ghosts and she said yes. My gran got upset and stopped talking about it. Death was never really talked about in our family. My gran said that the women in our family have a gift, and this gift has been in our family for many years. Then she said the best is yet to come, I did not understand what she meant".

"A few days went past and I convinced myself it was a dream. I remember going to bed and I felt an evil presence in my room again. I felt someone on my bed. I felt weak, and I tried to get up and put my light on but I couldn't move. I couldn't scream my body just would not move, I was so scared. I was on my back. The room was black and I felt that the small man was in my room again. He sat on top of me and was licking my face, I could hear myself saying yuk get off me and I

119

felt this 'thing' was trying to put me into a trance. I felt he was evil and all I could do was pray to God that this being would leave me alone. He was licking my face around my nose and mouth and I was finding it hard to breathe. I blacked out and the next morning when I woke I felt terrible violated".

"I did not say anything to my mother for fear of being accused of dreaming it all up. The attacks continued by this small man but he did not rape me, he was more interested in draining me of energy and restricting my breathing. One night I felt that I was being possessed, and had to fight it off me mentally, it was a fight I won. My mother reported seeing orbs and strange things happening around the house, and she said that she could hear her father's voice calling her name? My twin reported seeing a small boy on her bedroom window, she said he had yellow eyes and he was scratching the glass to get into her bedroom. I was feeling really ill mentally and physically and I tried to take my own life, I could not stand the torment any more. My attempt at an overdose and hanging failed. I told my mum that I wanted to go back to live with my father. I told my mother that I was being bullied at school which I was, and being visited by these things and that I just couldn't cope. I went to live with my father when I was 13. When I was 14, I saw my gran's face in my bedroom window she was smiling at me. It was my 14th Birthday. The phone rang and it was my sister to say that my gran had just died. I already knew".

"From the age of 14 to the age of 17, I did not experience anything paranormal. I thought I was free from it all. When I was 17, I moved into a flat with my boyfriend. I was looking out of the kitchen window one day and I saw my boyfriend's mother sitting in her car with a young man. She then came up to my flat and I asked her who the man was in the car with her. At which point she started screaming at me, and calling me a liar. She said that she had just been to her brother's grave to place flowers on it. She showed me a photo of her brother and it looked exactly like the man in the car! When I was 19, I moved into my first house with my partner and son. My partner *worked nights and we were getting our home straight. We kept ourselves to ourselves, everything was going fine until my neighbour started causing trouble for us because she was very jealous of us, we felt sorry for her. Well life was going fine until one night as I was going to bed, my son was crying, he did not want to sleep in his own bed, he was about 2 years old and he wanted to sleep in the top bunk bed. I kept checking on him every 10 minutes because I did not want him sleeping on the top bunk as I was worried that he was going to fall out. Anyway I was in bed when I heard a noise that sounded like a horse outside my bedroom window. This seemed out of place, as I have a garden outside my window. Well I then heard a noise coming from my son's room and I could not move. I had that draining feeling come over me again, I knew it was a ghost near me, and I could hear footsteps walking around my bed. I then saw the shape of a man, a big muscular man at the bottom of my bed, I blacked out. I then woke up to find this big cold man on top of me, he was raping me, he was very, very, cold. He had a very big penis and he was hurting me, so I tried to push him off me, he growled at me. I then went into a trance like state and I was trying to scream at him to get off me. I tried so hard, but could not get the words out. All I could think about was my son next door. I managed to start screaming and I felt my energy coming back, so I started fighting this man/beast, he was very muscular, like an ape man, he was very strange and cold and was trying to pin me to my bed and was continuing to try and rape me. He was biting and punching and grabbing my arms, he smelt so bad but I managed to kick him off. He made a big bang as he hit the floor. I looked at him, and he growled at me. He was getting really mad and was scaring me, but I was so angry with him. He jumped on top of me again and I saw his eyes were glowing red at that point I blacked out. My partner came back the next day saying he had to work longer. I was so angry with him".*

"My son was fine that night he said that he did not fall out the bunk bed, but said that he saw a little boy on the bottom of his bed who was scaring him. He said the boy had black eyes and cat teeth. It went quiet for a year or so, then my bed would

shake between 2am and 4am. Then I would feel my bed move behind me. I would have an arm around my chest to restrict my breathing. I would wake up to find scratches and bruises all over my body. Some nights my ankles were being grabbed and squeezed, and my arms were thrown above my head. I could see 3 small men all wearing hooded robes in my room. I got angry with the constant torment, so I started screaming at them, more so when they grabbed me, because they would hurt and leave me covered in bruises on my legs".

"In 1999 my son was born. In 2002 I had my daughter. The activity stopped, and I was able to live my life until 2009. One night my daughter went to the bathroom in the dark, she was screaming and ran down the stairs, something had scared her, and she said that she had seen a small boy with spiky hair in my bathroom. She told me he had yellow eyes. Her father said what a load of rubbish and that this house was not haunted. My daughter told me she would see this boy quite often, and felt he wanted to be her friend. Then one night (as I mentioned earlier) I saw a message on my bathroom wall it said, "I will accept a child, a next of kin". I was upset and angry I shouted "leave my children alone take me." I asked it for a sign, and I could hear scraping on my bathroom wall, like someone was scraping a shovel on the wall, then all the lights in the house and the street turned off. My family were all down stairs at the time and as I opened the bathroom door, I could hear a voice calling my name, so I ran down the stairs in the dark where I then felt something shove me, like a hand on my back when I was on the stairs. I have begged my partner for us to move house but he refuses, he said my house is not haunted and that I am crazy. My daughter hung white Jesus crosses on her bedroom wall after reporting the boy stroking her arm, this continued for a few months and she would see him at school also. She would also see this boy watching her in her bedroom".

(Author's Note) During the course of several days, Sharon and I exchanged further e-mails about the paranormal happenings that were going on in her house of which the following are but some.

"2010 I was setting my table for breakfast. I was downstairs alone, and my dog and cat were outside and my kids were upstairs getting ready. I could feel someone watching me, so I turned around out of curiosity, and saw a very tall thin man with a grey face in a hooded robe, he looked like a monk or grim-reaper. He was about 8 feet tall, I could not see his legs, and he looked as if he was floating. I also couldn't see his eyes or mouth, even although he was facing my direction. He was watching me and I managed to get a good description. I noticed a green glow coming from my door way. It was 8:00am, a Monday in March. I stood and watched him. I was about 7 feet away from him. We looked at each other and I felt scared. He then moved closer towards me and I started feeling ill. I said to him that I was not ready, and asked him to leave. At this point I ran into my kitchen to make a cup of tea, I kept telling myself that he was not real and that I was not seeing him. I looked into my living room and he was still there, so I ran upstairs to get my kids because I was afraid for them. I told my kids to hurry up and get changed so that I could get them out the house. My kids were refusing to get ready, and my son called me crazy and they would not listen to me. So I ran down stairs and looked in my living room and the man was gone, the green glow was also gone".

"My dog and cat act strange by my old doorway. I have noticed things happening around my house like windows and doors being opened, and I had a big black mark on my curtains but nobody knows who done it. I have heard footsteps and children's voices, and something was blowing on my face, but I could not see anyone. There have also been a lot of hot and cold spots around my house. I was cooking a roast one day when someone turned everything off. Taps and switches turn on and off by themselves. I thought I was going crazy. As I say, I have seen a small boy in my living room. Toys come on by themselves. I have seen orbs around my house and above my house, very pretty. Ghosts talk to me and smile at me because they know I can see them. I also have had a small girl wake me up, she grabs my arm and screams mum Sharon in my ear. I

123

have had a camera put up in my living room to try and catch something but all I got was white orbs. My partner said they were just dust particles and removed the camera. This house sometimes feels very evil and is not a home. I want so much to move house, but my partner refuses. All I can do is wait for my next encounter. I need help and I need to know why they have chosen me I have never used the Ouija board."

"I sometimes see shadows of people walking around my house and I feel hands touching me. My partner said that he has only ever had one encounter with something living here, and said that he was sitting watching T.V when he felt something jump up and sit by him, he thought it was our dog or the cat, but nobody was there. I would see faces of men women and children outside my room window. I smell smoke sometimes, and also smell rotten flesh. There is a smell near where I saw the man in my living room. Some days I smell perfume or cigarette smoke. I have been in bed and it sounded like my living room was full of people talking, and I could hear music, and as I go down the stairs to investigate, the sounds would stop. I have even been around to see if my neighbour was in, but her house was empty, and as I got back into bed, the noises started again. I have been in the bath and I have heard someone whistling a tune outside my bathroom door and when I investigate there is nobody there! I have a team in Sheffield interested in investigating my house".

(Author's Note). I asked Sharon if these bizarre events were most active at night or during the day or both, she replied.

"They are active both day and night but usually between the hours of 6:00pm and 8:00am mostly between March and September. Going by personal experiences, they are more likely to touch or attack me between 2:00am and 4:00am. Ghosts are all over the place, many look like normal everyday people to me. They make me go into a trance like state, this feels very strange like time stops. Maybe when I died when I was nine, it gave me this ability. I would like to have tests done on me to test my abilities. They are torments in my life to make me weak,

124

they feed off negative energy. Nobody can see them and I get cross not even my twin sister can see them.

"They are like naughty children, they thrive on attention. They can give me messages and show me things that I don't want to see. I know some ghosts will do anything just to be in a human body, some can get very jealous and try to take over my body. It is true when they say we are all spirits living a human life. They are more curious than anything. I told you that some of the spirits that visit me are not human. I feel like I am their guinea pig some days. I feel they have done something to me, so they can detect me anywhere I am in the world. I cannot hide from them. I tried to astral travel but I could not understand what I was seeing. I saw a double wooden bed and a yellow/gold item of clothing, weird. I do not seek spirit attention, I let them come to me. A few years ago I was tormented, I was shown a child in a basement in a place called Zagrilla. This is one of the reasons I made myself live with my father, it was for the safety of my family. After I snapped out of it, I felt very suicidal with the guilt. I could not live with myself. I am a very loving person, and for me to do something like that, or to hurt or harm my loved ones, well that was hell. The ghosts that visit me are real energy vampires. They restrict my breathing. They are real demons. Some people refer to these beings as Djinns. The small man that visits me is responsible for restricting my breathing and brainwashing and possession, he is about 3ft tall. The Incubus was a very big muscular man and was quite hairy. These all have the ability to make me weak and put me in a trance like state and they smell very bad. The only way I can describe them, is the smell of death, rotten flesh. When their eyes glow red, it is a sign they are seeking energy. I think they keep coming back to me because they are feeding off my energy. Normal spirits cannot do this. I am quite fond of the normal ghosts they are alright with me. I am worried for my daughter, she is 10 years old. I was 12 when my demons attacked me, but that was just a build up to my rapes".

"I have been doing a little research about my experiences, It states somewhere repeat attacks by Incubus can lead to a

125

person's death. People have asked me how I keep strong through all this, my answer is, I have no choice. I have sought help from Colin Fry, Barry Taff, Kerry Gaynor, Ian Tireney and Don Philips. (So far nothing) I have tried to have my house investigated by many teams here in the U.K. only to be let down, or to be told they can only help me if I pay for the help. I am a mother of three, I simply cannot afford to pay for people to investigate my house. I want to sit a lie detector test, and I want to have an exorcism taken out to see if that could help me. My partner is a sceptic and I have wanted the ghosts that visit me to touch him, but he only admits to that one time when he felt something jump and sit by him on the sofa"

"I have noticed the attacks only take place when I am in a room by myself, so I try to be with people most of the time. I have been in my kitchen, and I could feel a male presence of a normal ghost in the room with me. I have had a male ghost walk around my bed and get into my bed and just hold me in a loving way. I felt safe and protection coming from him. I don't know who he is. I was at Blackpool a few years ago, and a woman shouted at me and said, "Come and have your fortune read". I think many people are desperate just to get money off you, so I refused. As I walked past her, she shouted "He is in love with you" I said who is, and she said a tall dark stranger. I have seen a ghost dog in my living room and my son has seen it. It was chasing its tail".

"When I was 17 I was made to sit with the dying. My partner Patrick had a great aunt who lived next door, and she told me she would give me a sign if there is a life after death, I said "OK". Then, one day I was vacuuming my hall upstairs, and I felt someone slap the back of my hand. I knew it was Isa. Patrick came back and told me his aunt had died but I already knew. My spirits get me angry because I have asked for my gran to come and visit me, but she never does (Not all do when I ask!) My experiences are ruining my life and my relationship. I need help because I fear for my kids. I could not stand to see them go through anything that I have. The spirits visit me every 10 years or so. They have been with me 'all of my life' and I

know why. I am sharing some of my encounters with a group called Ammach, and there is also a film group in America who are interested in my story. Nobody in England seems to take my encounters seriously, and I am dreading the next encounter in 7 years time, not all of my experiences are nice. To have your memory wiped away only to remember things years later, freaks me out. My daughter thinks they have been taking her from the age of 8. The Shadow People are real, I see them, they look like monks/grim reapers. The greys and Shadow People are different beings but they work together. Well they did when I was 12 when they paralysed me and put an implant in my finger. I still have the scar to prove it. I have memories before I was a baby, and how I got here and before that also. I know that spirits, aliens and other beings come from the next plane and all work together, this is where you may be interested that UFO's are also involved. I have many answers about the next plane as I have been there a few times now. I know how to get back to this plane when I do die. I have had many out of body experiences and also near death experiences. I feel better now that my secret is out, I want so much to go back there. Thank you for reading this. I have to help others, this is my quest in this life. I just need to help get rid of the bad, the torment, and the evil, that are trying to stop us living in peace. I know if these beings are not stopped, they will torment us forever. The sceptics of this world will have it coming to them. I ask for help but deep down inside, I know that nobody here can help me. I should not be here I do not fit in here".

Sharon Cooper.

(Author's Note) Whilst I was in communication with Sharon, I had put a number of English paranormal researchers onto her to see if they could help, (As I had done with Patricia and Amanda) but sadly none of them could, well at least that is what Sharon told me! After a while my e-mails to her went unanswered, and the e-mail I have for her, comes back to me as undelivered. I just hope that this lady has found the peace and comfort that she so clearly needed.

My next case comes from a very dear friend of mine, Alyson Dunlop from Glasgow, who is now married to the lovely Ian Shanes. Ian was the psychic for our society SPI (Strange Phenomena Investigations) for many years, (indeed, still is) This account was also featured in my previous book, *'Paranormal Case Files of Great Britain (Volume 3)'* available on Amazon. But again, is featured here, as it is relevant to the discussion of the 'Hat Man' and 'Shadow People' in this book. It is worthy of note and comparison.

Alyson Dunlop Shanes.   *'Shadow Man Or Ghost'?*

"I saw a shadow person once when working in a private member's club at the University of Glasgow back in 2006. As you come into the building, there was a small set of stairs, with a hallway, and a bar to the left. Beyond the hallway there were stairs going up and stairs going down to a landing with some toilets. A colleague was sitting taking memberships. As I walked in, there was a shadow person standing in the corner at the foot of the stairs going down to the toilets. Whatever it/he/she was, definitely seemed to see me and crouched down in the corner. It looked like it did not want to be seen. My colleague asked me what was wrong, and when I told her, she said she had felt like she was being watched all morning. It freaked us both out a bit. I put it down to being the ghost of the building that the staff had often seen, felt or heard, and had affectionately named him, 'Hector', after the previous owner. I assumed I had just seen Hector. Maybe I had, but there was something different about him and it wasn't until I started hearing about Shadow People and seeing footage of them that I began to realise that what I had seen was far more like that, than a ghost".

(Author's Note) Alyson also had an encounter with the dreaded 'Hat Man' at home. Here is what she had to say.

"I have indeed seen the 'Hat Man'. I had chronic renal failure at the time and was waiting on a transplant. One night I turned over in bed and opened my eyes. There was a man

sitting beside me. He was wearing a trilby hat, which was slanted. He was side on, so I could only see the bottom half of his face which was a peculiar colour, creamy yellow-ish. I was really scared and the first thing that popped into my head was, Doctor Who. I am a big fan. At that time, The Doctor was Matt Smith, so I willed him to BE The Doctor, by repeating the phrase "You're The Doctor". As he began to turn his head, his face started morphing into a very good likeness of Matt Smith, but again I only ever saw the bottom half of his face. Anyway, I'd heard that people often see The 'Hat Man' when they are sick, and I also do find it weird that the Doctor in Doctor Who, is a fan of hats! Some have said they would have associated the hat with Odin, so that could be another avenue to look into, as Odin is a god of healing, but also a god who is a psychopomp. As for how it ended, I just passed out and went into a sleep. When I woke the next morning he was gone"

Alyson Dunlop

(Author's Note). Alyson mentions above the word 'psychopomp'. Well, that font of knowledge which is Wikipedia, tells us, (and I quote) 'Psychopomps are creatures, spirits, angels, or deities in many religions, whose responsibility is to escort newly deceased souls from Earth to the afterlife. Their role is not to judge the deceased, but simply to guide them. Appearing frequently on funerary art, psychopomps have been depicted at different times and in different cultures as anthropomorphic entities, horses, deer, dogs, ravens, crows, vultures, owls, sparrows, and cuckoos. When seen as birds, they are often seen in huge masses, waiting outside the home of the dying. (unquote)

Our next case comes from another friend of mine, and someone who certainly has witnessed more strange things than the ordinary man in the street. His name is Bill Rooke, but is fondly known as 'Alien Bill'. In this account, Bill tells us about his encounter with a 'Shadow Person', which, as you will see, was quite vicious and none too pleasant. This event took place in a pub car park in the town of York in England.

Bill Rooke.   *'I Was Attacked By A Shadow Person'!*

"After a Saturday evening in my local on the 27th May 2016, I left by the car park side entrance around 12-30am. Just outside the doors, I was greeted by some white orbs about the size of crown green bowling balls. These have appeared to me on many occasions, but this time something seemed amiss. The orbs were darting about in a tight formation and seemed agitated. I spoke to them as I often do and said, "I am coming to my field to do some filming and will see you there". They then just disappeared, and I headed off over the car park to my bike, puzzled over what had just occurred. Having arrived at my bike, I put my haversack down that I carry my photographs of my cosmic and paranormal images plus camera equipment, and began taking my bike lock off. I then sensed something strange happening behind me next to a very long bush about 25 foot long and 8 feet high. As I turned around, coming through this bush, was a jet black human form, a shadow man, and not translucent. Now I am wondering, did the orbs know there was something lurking in the car park waiting for me and they were there darting about trying to warn me? I can only guess at that".

"This entity was around 6 feet 6 inches tall, and moved towards me in an intimidating manner. I jumped back in shock but was not afraid, as I had seen a similar entity before, but was just annoyed that it had sneaked up on me. 7 months before this, a similar shadow man looking just like this, appeared at the end of my bed in the early hours, just the same, a black shadow shape of a human form. On this occasion I could see it silhouetted against my window and it somehow was applying pressure on me. I sat up after telling it off in no uncertain terms that it didn't belong here. It then disappeared. While this was happening, my little dog Rocky was fast asleep at the end of the bed, and my wife lying next me didn't stir a jot. That surprised me. Now this fellow in the car park which looked the same, meant business, and I stood back prepared for what was about to happen. As the shadow moved towards me, it held its massive hands out as if it was going to grab me, instead I was thrown

130

backwards with my Ray Bann sunglasses that I always wear, being pulled off me at the same time. Luckily, I landed on some grass and, very annoyed, told the shadow being off, that it had better not broken my shades. Getting up I picked up my glasses which were OK and said jokingly, "Right, have you been working out at the gym fella". I then took my camera from my haversack and set it on flash mode to get evidence, but nothing appeared. Then I tried without the flash, still nothing. I couldn't understand when I could see this thing with my naked eye, and yet I couldn't get an image on camera of it. I had one last go as it moved towards me shuddering as it came forward, and tried video mode, still nothing, so I gave up on that and concentrated on the battle ahead. Again, as it neared me with its massive outstretched arms, my feet lifted off the grass, my glasses were pulled off again 'without it actually touching me!' and I was thrown backwards once again, landing next to a tree, where this time my head hit the ground first, and I suffered a mild whiplash effect from the fall".

"This time I crawled around on the grass until I had my glasses back on which luckily had not broken. Now I need some evidence of this encounter or a witness, so I got my mobile phone out and phoned Nick Kyle in Glasgow who investigates the paranormal. It was in the early hours when I rang him, and he heard me telling the entity off as he answered the phone, and at first Nick thought that someone was threatening him. He was very concerned what was happening to me when he realised it was his friend Alien Bill from York taking on a shadow being. After giving him a rough idea what was happening, I still had to confront the shadow being, so I put my phone down on my bag which I left on by accident and which Nick could still hear me telling the shadow being that I would get rid of it. By this time, I had lost track of time and found out later that I was there much longer than I first realised. Standing now within 7 feet of shadow man, I yelled at him again, "You do not belong here" as it just stood vibrating in a strange manner. At this point, it moved backwards into the bush that it first appeared from, fading away as it did so. Boy what a relief I felt, but at the same time I felt empathy for it, as it felt lost in some way to me,

131

even after it had given me a bit of a bashing. I wish my camera could have picked something up, as many years before, I did manage to get pictures of Shadow People from another realm, but they are all flat on the floor not upright like this one. Another twist to this strange tale, is that after I told my wife about this encounter, she told me that about a week earlier when she was in bed around 12-30am, a shadow being appeared to her outside our bedroom window for 2 to 3 minutes. Firstly, she thought it was her imagination and shut her eyes, then opened them again to see this dark shape was still there hanging down from the roof. These shadow folks have been seen by many people globally, some wearing hats and others clothing. The ones I have seen, appeared as a jet black naked human form with no hair, and never seem too friendly. There is no doubt these shadow folks exist. I believe there are many types from other dimensions and they are not all bad, some seem to have the hump with humanity however".

Regards, Bill Rooke.

Now that wasn't the only time that Bill had encountered a 'Shadow Person', five years earlier, Bill not only witnessed a 'Shadow Person', but actually took a photograph of it as well, as he briefly mentioned above. Here is what he had to say.

"While in my front garden on the 4th of September 2009, around 3-30am, I captured on camera, a shadow entity. At the time I was trying to film light beings and orbs next to a large bush in my neighbours garden. This I have done over many years. While facing the bush, this shadow entity was flat on the pebble stones and came from behind me and seemed to want to join me at what I was doing. Not totally surprised by this, I did jokingly say to it, "Hello have you come for a bit of a nosey". I then turned around to film it further, and the photograph that I took, you can see my feet pointing towards it. The camera cord can also be seen hanging in front of the camera". (see photographic section)

"While taking these images, a translucent red orb appears with it and coloured the camera cord a reddish colour. The

camera was on flash mode, and the light didn't seem to penetrate into the shadow being and show up the pebbles underneath it. When departing after these pictures were taken, the entity backed away slightly and vanished in an instant. I do believe that not all of the shadow folk are bad, but some of course are not too good to be involved with. When it first approached me at the bush, I did get a creepy sensation, but felt no energy from it apart from that, and I had no verbal communication or telepathic message. These to me seem to be of interdimensional origin, but we are of course in a cosmic college and still on many learning curves. The likes of 'Hat Man' and many other visitors can fit into this category of folk from other realms".

Regards, Bill Rooke.

In an e-mail communication with Bill, he assured me that no one was near him at the time that this 'shadow' loomed in front of him, it was purely him, and this Shadow Entity.

Darren W. Ritson. *'The Silhouette Boy'*

The following disturbing ghostly account, comes from the pen of my good friend, a fellow researcher and author, Darren W. Ritson. Darren discusses a few strange events, that for all intents and purposes could well be linked. They occurred to his father, Walter Ritson in the early 1970s, and then to Darren himself also in the 1970s, and again some years later in the 1980s. Darren states.

"My earliest recollection of paranormal activity was around the age of ten. It was when I was sent to bed, and when I was the only one in the house upstairs. My brother, Gary, was three years older than I, and he was allowed to stay up a little longer than I was. This really irritated me, because deep down, I knew I did not want to be upstairs on my own. As I lay in bed, trying to get to sleep with the landing light left on 'of course'! I often heard the sound of the stairs creaking, as if someone was creeping up them. Now, most people would say that old houses creak anyway, and they do. The difference however, is that it

seemed to me that every creak or noise the stairs made, coincided with what noise would have been made if somebody were actually ascending the staircase. You see, some stairs made some recognisable and distinguishing noises and some stairs did not make any noise at all".

"I became convinced that someone was creeping up the stairs. As I lay there frozen in my bed, the noises on the staircase become louder, as though whoever, or whatever was making its accent, was getting closer to my room. The noises kept on coming as I became more and more frozen with fear, until they reached the top. I thought it may have been my mother or father checking up on me to make sure I was indeed asleep, but on calling out to them, I had no response. That frightened me even more. I soon began to realise that whoever or whatever was present, was now standing behind my bedroom door, and this was where it always seemed to stop, every time it happened. Then, as I was lying there in total silence, I could feel and hear my heart thundering furiously along with the distinctive noise of slow breathing that was emanating from behind the door. At this point as I was so petrified, I screamed out for my parents. I subsequently heard the downstairs door open and can clearly remember hearing the voices of my father, mother and brother at the bottom of the stairs near to the living room, which clearly indicated to me, that it could not have been a family member creeping about, they were clearly downstairs in the living room. This happened on countless occasions, and I am convinced I heard what I heard. I was wide-awake at the time, and I can still remember this as if it were yesterday. What it was, or whoever it was, I never really found out, but it had a profound effect on me and it is something I won't ever forget".

"My father had always told me about a young lad that once lived in my old house, in fact; he used to occupy the bedroom that I actually used as a child growing up, before my parents moved into the house. I know this because my mother and my grandmother lived in the house across the street opposite, before my mother married my father. One day, this youngster came out from his house, and for reasons unknown, perhaps he was bored, stood in my grandmother's passageway at the bottom of her stairs (as the front door was always left open)

134

and began to play with the light switch flicking it on and off rapidly creating a strobe like effect. He was soon scolded by my grandmother for he could have blown the fuses in the entire house; or worse, he could have electrocuted himself. A few hours later he was seen again, only this time he was making his way behind his house and down onto the old railway line that was then an electric railway, where sadly he was electrocuted and died. When I was a child growing up in the 1970s, the railway line was still there, but was not an electric one, with trains still operating on it. I often had to jump off the tracks when I heard a train coming and often times stood alongside it as it trundled past. How times have changed, for the better I must add. Health and safety in those days had a lot to be desired".

"Many years later, when 'we' occupied the house, my dad would hear footsteps in his bedroom from the living room downstairs, which was directly underneath his bedroom, which in turn, overlooked the old railway line. Presuming it was either my brother or I out of our beds messing about, he would shout up the stairs to tell us to 'get back into bed'. He would receive no answer, and all would fall quiet. On one occasion, he raced up the stairs to find that we were indeed sound asleep in our beds. He meandered through into his bedroom and looked out of the window, whereupon he noticed what appeared to be a young boy sauntering about on the line, and in the dark. Thinking to himself, 'it's a bit late for a youngster to be out on his own', he watched him walk off and out of sight and thought no more of it until he realised a few days later, that the night he saw the young boy on the railway lines, was immediately after hearing the pattering of footfalls in his room from downstairs, and in actual fact, it was the anniversary of the tragic youngsters death! Make of that what you will. Was the ghost of the young boy pitter-pattering his way around the top floor of the house before being seen at the spot where he was electrocuted all those years ago? An interesting postscript ensues".

"One hot summers evening back in the 1980's when I was a grumpy skinny teenager, I decided to retire to bed. After I had lain down, I slowly began to heat up, so I took off my t-shirt in

an attempt to cool off before I went to sleep. I soon nodded off, but during the night I woke up, and for some reason I felt really anxious. I then noticed standing in my doorway, the shadow or silhouette of a young boy roughly about ten years old. All I wanted to do at that point, was reach across for the t-shirt, which was on the floor, and put it on, (never mind the fact that there was what appeared to be the ghost of a young boy at the door of my room). This I did, and for about two minutes I lay in my bed and stared at this small silhouette of a boy. The next thing I remember I was waking up in the morning. I must have fallen back to sleep. My first thoughts were, 'What a strange dream I had', until I got out of my bed and realised that my t-shirt was back on, only back to front and inside out. So, I did get up in the night and put my t-shirt back on, which raises the question, why? Was the boy really in my doorway after all? I can't say for sure, it may have been the ghost of the young boy who once lived in my old house, or it may have been a dream. However, since my father used to hear what he described as 'anomalous footfalls' in the house when my brother and I were asleep, I am inclined to think it may have been the ghost. Nevertheless it was quite disturbing for me thinking how vivid the whole episode was. I felt that the apparition may well have been looking at me in my bed, and could have been thinking, 'Who are you and what are you doing in my bedroom?' Perhaps it was also the 'shadow boy' that I had heard on many occasions making his way up the stairs too? So many questions, and never enough answers. Needless to say it has stayed with me all of these years and is one of the reasons I began to eventually investigate ghosts and hauntings".

Darren Ritson. *'The South Shields Poltergeist Shadow Man'*

Darren was also kind enough to supply me with information on an incident relating to a 'Shadow Man' that appeared in a famous poltergeist case that both he and his friend Michael J. Hallowell investigated. Here is what Darren had to say about that incident.

"*During the famous South Shields poltergeist case and its investigation of 2005/2006 that was thoroughly researched and documented by myself Darren W. Ritson and Michael J. Hallowell, at the Tyneside home of Marc Karlsonn and Marianne Peterworth (pseudonyms), the poltergeist seemingly took on an appearance in a number of different ways. On one occasion for example, it materialised itself as an old apparitional man. In the early stages of the infestation however, it took the form of a so called playmate of young Robert (Marianne's son, also a pseudonym), calling himself 'Sammy'. However, on one particular night, the poltergeist, entity, or whatever it was, decided to show itself in a much more harrowing and sinister way in the form of a 'Shadow Man'. On the evening in question, Michael Hallowell had been telephoned by a much troubled and quite hysterical Marianne, after her partner Marc had been seemingly viciously cut and scratched by the entity not long after retiring to their beds. Michael quickly got dressed, grabbed his bag with his dictation device and his camera, and made off hastily in a taxi to Lock Street to offer his assistance in what way he could. Upon entering the 'haunted house' Michael was greeted with a somewhat relieved Marc and Marianne, and began to question the two householders about what had transpired. During the course of his stay that night, a number of other incidents occurred that was verified and documented, including a second 'scratch' attack on Marc, which Michael was able to film while it occurred, followed by a barrage of objects being hurled around as if with unseen hands. If that wasn't bad enough, during an examination of the upper floors of the house, they found that little Robert's bedroom had been completely turned upside down; the bed, which was normally tucked neatly into the corner against the wall, was now in the middle of the floor, toys were strewn all over, the furniture had been tipped over, and a urine stain was left on the floor*".

"*It was here, on the upper floor, where the intense paranormal activity drew to a harrowing end (at least for the time being) culminating in the sighting of what can only be described as a human shaped black shadow as it marched from one room into the next. With kind permission, the following paragraph has been lifted and reproduced from Darren W. Rit-*

son's latest 3rd edition release of the book detailing the entire case, *The South Shields Poltergeist: One families Fight Against an Invisible Intruder (Ritson, 2020)*".

"*As Mike took another photograph, something else moved just within his peripheral vision. It was on the landing just outside of Robert's room. Marianne saw it too, and screeched. The entity strode slowly but purposefully from the bathroom and walked across the landing into the master bedroom. As it passed the door to Robert's room, it paused momentarily, and stared icily at Mike. It was large, maybe two metres in height and midnight black. It was a three-dimensional silhouette that radiated sheer evil. It had no eyes, and yet it was staring. Its face, devoid of all features, was nevertheless menacing. Mike stared back, and then calmly spoke into his digital recorder.*

"*For the benefit of the tape, something, or someone, has just walked from the bathroom into Marianne and Marc's room...*" "*Woah...!*" *said Marianne again,* "*Did you see someone there...?*" "*Yes I did...just like a black shape...but it's gone now.*"

"*Now Marianne was really frightened, and the situation wasn't helped when some toy bells belonging to Robert vacated their normal home in his toy hammock and, jingling merrily, presented themselves at Marianne's feet. The room then went icy-cold*".

Darren W. Ritson.

(Author's Note) It's not surprising how I, as the author of this book, simply love this subject. Yes the story above is frightening and alarming to the family that went through it, but let us not forget, there are dedicated researchers out there, the likes of Darren W. Ritson, and his colleague Michael Hallowell who can offer some help and guidance along the way to those people, like the family above, who had to suffer those horrible events. We now move onto another account from a well known Scottish psychic by the name of Lee Dunn, he too, has a story to share.

Lee Dunn. *"I Am Here To Witness"!*

Hi Malcolm

"As a Spiritual Medium, I've encountered many strange things over the years. I have a scientific and technological background and I'm a Senior Fellow of the Higher Education Academy, and so my professional career has taught me to apply logic to situations, so any information that I share, I do so with caution, and with a genuine interpretation on what I experienced. But I do accept that the world around us is complex and still to be understood on many levels. During the onset of the Coronavirus Pandemic, I felt myself pulled in many directions. I'd been spending a lot of time speaking with people who felt lost and alone during an unprecedented time of isolation. Over the course of a number of weeks, strange things were happening around me. I'd made a series of public predictions in late December 2019, for the year ahead and I'd long since seen the world in chaos around us. The magnitude of the situation and the pressure that I endured was enormous. I was receiving several messages a day from people seeking guidance and help at a time when I also felt vulnerable".

"In June 2020, I found my sleep to be disturbed by dreams of strange, supernatural beings. I couldn't easily explain who or what they were, and I'm not especially religious, so I dismissed them as angelic beings and thought nothing more about it. I'd experienced some darker things in the past too, but not for a long time. I thought about these beings again when I went through a very vivid meditation where I'd floated up through the sky and found myself on what I can best describe as a different place, which consisted of a large lake and crystal like plants. My own guides had told me that I was in the presence of Master Guides, and that I had a role to play in helping people through the months ahead. It was so profound, that I'd written and published a book about it at the time".

"During the summer, I awakened in the early hours, soaked in sweat and aware that I was being studied. My wife slept peacefully beside me, oblivious to the figure standing at the

139

bottom of the bed. He was over six feet tall, wearing a long dark coat and a wide brimmed hat. I could not see his face, which was in shadows, but I knew instinctively that he was staring at me. I've had similar things happen in the past, when spirit had visited during the night. Often, this happens just before I'm about to do a reading for someone, or when I'm about to go onto the platform for charity or for a Spiritualist Church. I'm naturally open to spirit, but this was the first time that I had encountered this man in a hat, and his energy felt very different. Almost elemental or non-human like. I knew right away that there was something special about him. I didn't feel any sense of threat or malevolence from him. But neither did I feel that he was good or benevolent. I firmly believe that evil exists in humanity, but he was different. He felt neutral. I asked him who he was and why he was there, but at first he did not speak or attempt to communicate in any way. The whole episode lasted only a few minutes and then he was gone. As he faded, I heard a reply like a distant whisper in the wind. 'I am here to witness,' he said. To witness what, I did not know. I suspect it was a result of the pandemic and the increase in lost souls seeking my advice and support. I felt that something was at play, and that this man had somehow come to me because I was active in trying to help people. I'd long ago phrased a term 'spiritual convergence' meaning that people from diverse backgrounds come together, often under tragic circumstances such as war, murder, tragic accidents or pandemics".

"The days that followed were even stranger, with many connections and synchronicities happening around me. On two occasions, I'm convinced that I saw him again, quietly watching me from a distance, like a stranger out of time or from any place. It's my belief that the 'Hat Man' somehow defies our known laws of nature and physics and travels to see things happen to and around people. It's an encounter I will never forget and I'm sure it's only a matter of time before I cross paths with him again".

Lee Dunn

My good friend Kathy Cogliano from Massachusetts USA, who herself is a gifted psychic, sent me her account of witnessing several 'Shadow People'. Here is what she had to say.

Kathy Cogliano. *'Shadow People Encounter at Butterfly Hill Farm'.*

"I met the owners of Butterfly Hill Farm; Claudia and Bruce while visiting my friends William and Clare in Nashville in June of 2014. Claudia and Bruce invited a group of us to come to their farm and join them for dinner. Butterfly Hill Farm is a beautiful farm, located high up in the Smokey Mountains of Tennessee. When we arrived, we had a tour of the property the views were absolutely stunning".

"I felt called to take a walk in the woods surrounding the farm, walking on an old Native American trail. I was joined by two friends and we set out to explore the trail and surrounding wooded area. It wasn't long into our hike that I heard some funny whistles and clicking sounds all around us, I asked the other two guys if they heard the clicking and whistles and both said no. All of a sudden, I could 'see' a group of Native American men come running through the woods as though they were chasing something, there had to have been about eight men all making these whistle and clicking noises. I was the only one who could 'see' and 'hear' them. I told the guys what was happening, and they were transfixed as I told them what I was seeing. I could even feel a rush of air as they ran by us! We continued our exploration of the trail. We came upon the remains of a very old man made high rock wall. It almost seemed it could have been a foundation. Most of it was intact, some of it had crumbled. We stopped and talked about what this might have been. Rich, a history teacher, thought that it might be the remains of some kind of fort. All of a sudden spirit showed me how the wall was made; I 'saw' a group of black slaves working in teams building the wall with large stones, fitting each together, working with tools chipping the stone as needed. At one point I could 'hear' them singing a song as they worked. It was glimpse of a moment in time".

"We made our way back to the farmhouse with the rest of our group. As we stepped onto the porch, Bruce the owner was on the porch and greeted us. Rich proceeded to tell him about what we experienced in the woods. Bruce then told us that they have felt the Native spirits around the farm in the past. He confirmed there was a slave trade industry in the hills of the area. Spirit showed me glimpses of the history of this beautiful land. We went into the house and all settled in to enjoy a wonderful dinner. The sun was setting with spectacular colours as the evening sky turned black. We were all gathered in the big area of the kitchen and great room. I was standing with a group of friends, with my friend Loretta to my left. I was facing the far wall, when I saw movement. I looked, and couldn't believe what I was seeing. A group of people in shadows, moving as though walking around, yet there wasn't anyone standing near that wall at the time to cast a shadow, yet the shadows of people were on the wall moving! I looked at Loretta and I said; "Do you see these Shadow People on the wall?" She nodded yes, and we both just watched as these Shadow People moved about slowly. I had the sense that they were Native American, she agreed. (Note: Loretta is a spiritual medium, healer) We didn't make a big deal of what we were seeing to the rest of the group, looking back we didn't say anything to our group as to not disrupt the gathering and perhaps cause any fear".

"Later in the evening I went up to Claudia and Bruce and told them what Loretta and I saw, and they said they had seen this group of Shadow People recently. They asked me if I sensed if they were peaceful? I said we felt they were peaceful and benevolent, and I sensed they were protectors of the land as this was their home also. Claudia and Bruce agreed, they felt they were peaceful and watched over the farm".

Kathy Cogliano

One of my friends on Facebook, Aaron Flanagan, sent me his account of witnessing a 'Shadow Person' wearing a Fedora type hat in his bedroom some years ago. Here is what he had to say.

Aaron Flanagan. 'The Standing, Staring, Shadow Hat Person'

"The first time was when I was laying in bed. The house was tall (ground, 1st and 2nd floor) in the town of Dedridge which is near the larger town of Livingston in West Lothian Scotland. I had not long moved bedrooms to the top of the house. My father's new partner had come into a sum of money and she had spent a lot of it redecorating and rearranging the house to match her own tastes and not my late mother's. It was within the first week of being in that bedroom. I was laying in bed facing the bedroom door which was about 5 meters away from me. I wasn't asleep, and I couldn't get to sleep, but I had my eyes closed. I opened them for no particular reason that I can remember (I certainly didn't feel like I was being watched) but when I opened them, in the darkness, I could see someone standing in front of my door. At first I felt no fear because I automatically assumed it was my father standing outside in the hallway checking in on me. But with my bedroom being at the top of the house, and it being a somewhat creaky house built in the 1960s, I was surprised I hadn't heard him. Then, as my eyes adjusted to the darkness, I realised that the figure wasn't standing outside in the hallway. My bedroom door had recently been painted white instead of the old dark brown wood, and as my eyes adjusted more, I could see that whoever was standing there, was actually standing inside my bedroom in front of the closed door, of which I could now make out the handle and door frame. I could also, by this point, make out that the shadowy figure 'wasn't my father at all', because it was too tall and too slim, and was also wearing a hat (which I used to describe as being like Freddy Krueger's) something my father nor anyone I knew, would wear".

"My eyes were wide open by now, unblinking and staring, trying to make out any details, but only seeing the flat, subtle, dark grey/black of the silhouette. It never moved, and I heard no noise. I still didn't feel at this point that I was being watched. I almost felt like I had stumbled upon it. All I remember is holding my breath, and slowly raising my duvet to

143

cover my eyes, and eventually my whole head. It was still standing there the last I saw of it. I must have eventually fallen asleep. But the next morning, when my father woke me for school, I told him about it. He didn't believe me, and said that the ghost stories my late mother and siblings used to tell me about the house (he and my mum were separated before her death, so he wasn't there to experience the strange goings on) had gotten to me, and having a bedroom beside the attic must've spooked me. To this day, 17 years later, I know I didn't imagine it, and I know it wasn't a dream. It was the first thing I had ever seen in that house (I'd heard and felt a lot, as had others) but unlike other family members I had never 'SEEN' anything until that night".

Aaron Flanagan

Another dear friend from Facebook, Joanne Cochrane, wrote to tell me about her own experiences with 'Shadow People.

Joanne Cochrane.   *'My encounter with Shadow People'.*

"I had this experience about 10 years ago, (2011) at my house in Armadale, West Lothian, Scotland. Over the course of a week, I had the sensation of not being alone, and that someone was watching me, then one night, just as I had got into bed, I felt the bottom of my bed give in, as if someone had sat down next to my feet. I did all the usual things, get up put light on, check that no one was in the room (I lived alone, and at that time with no pets) there was no one in the room. The following night, I had the same experience, got in bed, and a couple of minutes later, the bed gave in. This time it felt heavier, if that makes sense. Again I got up checked the room, and nothing".

"A few nights later, I had the most terrifying experience. On getting into bed I felt I wasn't alone, I had this overwhelming feeling that someone was in the room with me, I felt that I was being watched from the right hand corner of my bedroom. I tried to shrug this off and closed my eyes. Within minute's, my eyes were wide open, and I could see this shadow figure out the corner of my eye moving closer and closer to my bed. I was terrified, but I couldn't scream, it felt like forever but within a

few seconds I was able to move and get out my bed. I had this experience at least four times over the course of months, each one being more terrifying than the other. I did some research on sleep paralysis, and found all the usual stuff about not sleeping on your back etc, and decided that each time I was going to bed, I would prepare myself, and hopefully be able to deal with these Shadow People (by this time there was more than one). I prepared a ritual, every night I would call in my guides, angels, guardians whatever you want to call them. I would say a prayer and meditate. I did this for days. Then one evening I had that familiar feeling of being watched. I continued my ritual, filled my bedroom with white light, then got into bed with the intentions of a good night's sleep. Then the bed gave in, I felt a deep dreading of danger. I wanted to get out of bed but couldn't move, I couldn't scream, all I could do was watch, as these Shadow People moved closer and closer to me. Then to the left of me appeared what I can only describe as a huge black doglike creature, this animal placed its two front paws on my bed (like a dog would do) showing its teeth and snarling, not at me, but at whatever was in the room with me. I was absolutely petrified. It happened so fast, then it was over. The strangest thing is afterward I didn't feel afraid, I felt emotional, and cried for days but never felt afraid".

"It was months later, through working with a Shaman, that I discovered this doglike animal was in fact an accumulation of my spirit guides, angels and guardians that I had summoned for help. Was this a fight between dark and light taking place in my bedroom? I truly believe so. Although I continue to see Shadow People, I have never had this experience again in my bedroom".

Joanne Cochrane.

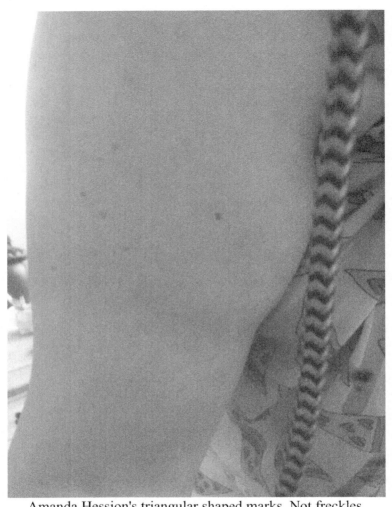
Amanda Hession's triangular shaped marks. Not freckles.
(c) Amanda Hession

Another Reptilian creature (c) Patricia Hession

Coloured balls of light appeared in front of Patricia and
Amanda, moving from left to the right then just vanished.
(c) Patricia Hession.

The 'Hat Man' as seen by both Amanda and Patricia.
(c) Patricia Hession

Another 'Hat Man' drawing as seen by both Patricia and Amanda. (c) Patricia Hession.

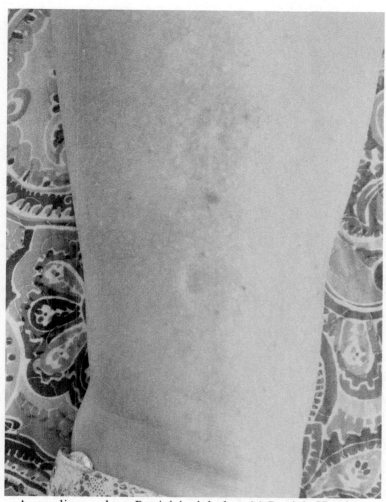
A peculiar mark on Patricia's right leg. (c) Patricia Hession.

A mock up of the amber lights and large orb seen above
Patricia's garage. (c) Patricia Hession.

Mock up of UFO witnessed by Pat and Amanda. Edgmore Park

Patricia and Amanda Hession

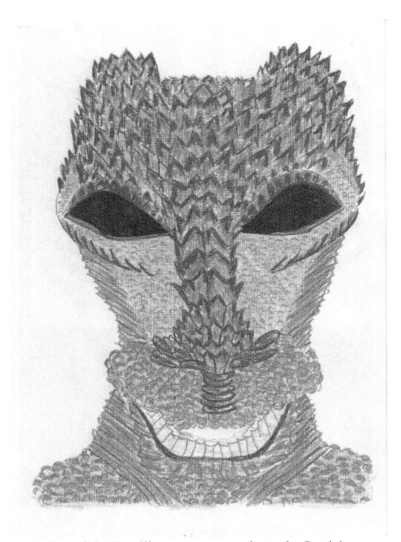

One of the Reptilian creatures, as drawn by Patricia.
(c) Patricia Hession

Patricia and Amanda sat on this swing to observe a UFO hovering above Edgmore Park. (c) Patricia Hession.

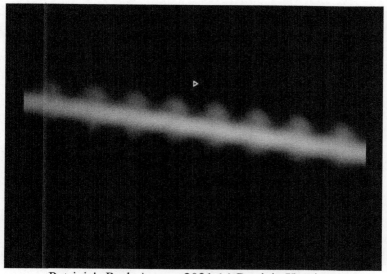

Patricia's Rod. August 2021 (c) Patricia Hession.

Patricia's sketch of the house in Baden Baden Germany.
(c) Patricia Hession.

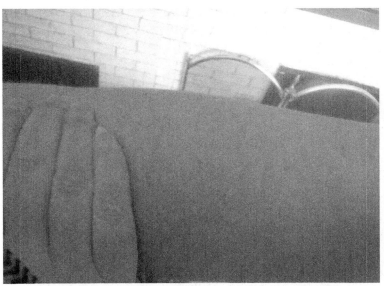

Strange marks on Patricia's arm. (c) Patricia Hession.

The large gilded mirror that was thrown off the wall by an unseen force. (c) Patricia Hession.

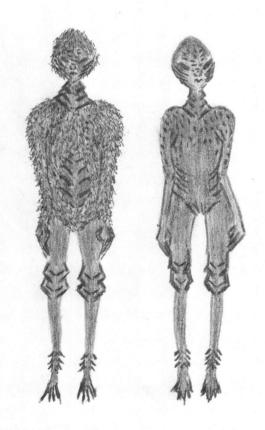

These 'beings' were only around 15 cms in height and appeared
in Patricia and Amanda's bedroom. (c) Patricia Hession

Interview with Author Natalie Osborne Thomason.

I had asked another good friend of mine, English woman Natalie Osborne Thomason who has written books about ghosts and the paranormal, if she had any Shadow People or 'Hat Man' stories that she could relate to me, stories that she may have picked up during her own ghostly investigations. Needless to say she did, and on the 24th of July 2021, I proceeded to do a telephone interview with her about them. The following is but part of a more lengthy interview.

(MR)   "Firstly, thanks for speaking with me Natalie. Can I ask you right at the start, when did the paranormal all start for you"?

(NT)   "Well I've written four books on ghosts and hauntings, but I wasn't aware of Shadow People per se, until it started to happen to me and my family. I went to Stratford Upon Avon, about ten years ago (2011) And I visited a house that was terribly haunted.   And the chap said that since he moved into the house, horrible things have happened, and could I move it on, or give him some advice. It was a friend of mine who put me in touch with this young couple, so I went along to the flat and had a look around, and in a mirror in the house, which was very old and which I thought was an antique, I saw an image of a man hanging! It was just for a split second. And I thought, 'Oh my God, this is awful' and I didn't quite know what to say to the couple. But I said to the guy, "Can you tell me where you got the mirror from"? And he said that he got it from the pub where he worked, I think he said the Elm Tree pub, but I could be wrong. He said that they were closing it down, and that he was told that he could take what he wanted, to which I said, "Well I've found the cause of your haunting, it's the mirror". At that he said, "But you haven't even looked around the flat yet", at which point I said that I would in a moment. And there were all these dirty hand prints on the wall, and the couple didn't have dirty jobs. It was almost like a coal miner had touched the walls, and they had left a couple of hand prints for me to see before they scrubbed them off. Anyway, they

159

begged me to take the mirror away with me, which I did, I put it in my car. It was so big that I had to pull some of the seats down just to get it in, it was so huge. Before I left however, we all held hands and asked whatever or whoever was in the flat to depart, and I told them to put salt in the four corners and light a candle. I've come across haunted objects many times, and I usually bring them home with me to get them away from the home that is causing problems. So I was driving back from Stratford Upon Avon, back to Northampton, and all the while I could hear a man saying, "F**k off, you bitch, you cow, what are you doing" And the smell of cigarette smoke in the car was so strong. I was thinking, 'Oh my God, what have we got here'? And I said, "Oh shut up, you don't frighten me, just shut your gob" Anyway, I didn't think too much of it. I put the mirror by the side of my dining table, and I covered it up with a cloth, hoping that I didn't have to look at it and see that image of the man hanging. When the mirror was all covered, I asked the man that I had spoken to in the flat if someone had hung themselves in that pub that he had worked at, where he had got the mirror, and he said, yes, there had been a hanging of a man. And he asked me why I was asking him that, and he freaked out when I told him that I had seen an image of a man hanging in the mirror. Anyway, my daughter came down in the morning, and she didn't know that I had been out the previous day and what I was doing, and she said, "Mum, last night there was a man in the room, there was this shadow, and it was horrible. And I said, 'Really"? And she said "yes". So I said to her that it must have been a bad dream, and she looked over next to my dining table and said, "What's that thing there, it's not haunted is it"? I said "No". And she said, "Yes it is", and I said, "Oh alright then, it is"! Then I said that I will do something with it, but as yet I didn't know what I would do with it. And If I hadn't seen that hanging man in the mirror, I would have been tempted to put it on one of the walls of my house. But it had a nasty feeling about it, a nasty vibe. Anyway, I kept the mirror for a few days, but the whole time that the mirror was here, my daughter kept seeing shadow things in her room. And at that time she worked in a home for disturbed children with behavioural problems up the road, it was quite an old house. *And on one occasion when the mirror was still in the house, she was on a shift and she had to sleep there, and there was a thunderstorm, and I believe that Shadow People and the 'Hat Man' are connected to thunderstorms as well. And she said that there was a strike of lightning, and she and this young girl saw, within this strike of lightning, appear a man with a hat, and they both screamed and they ran up the stairs, even although the strike of lightning was outside. And I think that Becky said that it was the same man that had been in her room. And she said mum, its followed me to my work. And it disturbed her so much, that she had to have two weeks off work, where she went to the doctor's and was on anti-depressants for a while. She had actually said to the doctor, please don't think that I am crazy, but my mum brought back a haunted mirror etc etc, and the doctor to his credit said, that my daughter did appear very upset and that 'he believed her'. Then this 'thing' started appearing in my room, it wasn't the 'Hat Man', it was a shadow".*

(MR) "*So, what to your knowledge actually happened to that mirror?*"

(NT) "*Well I've had a couple of e-bay accounts, and e-bay can sometimes close your account if they don't agree with something you've sold. I also had several haunted dolls that I came across, or was given, and I put them on there, and they closed my account. Whether somebody complained about the haunted mirror, I don't know. So I don't know what happened to that mirror. What I think though, is that they probably did smash it, or they dumped it somewhere. The mirror is what drew that 'man' to my house, and my daughter's fear drew the 'Shadow People'. So it is a consequence of events you know.*
"*I've never been frightened of ghosts. I've been all around the world ghost hunting. I've investigated over 100 cases, I've done so much, and I'm proud that I have never been frightened. In fact, I've been bitten, I've been scratched, I've had things thrown at me, I've been threatened, they have said, "Die Bitch" and things like that. And I've said, "Oh whatever, just do your worst". But, I started to have this terrible fear. There was this*

'thing' in my room. It was usually standing in the corner of my room. At the time I had a four poster bed which was open at the top, and this 'thing' was like on the ceiling. And I could tell that it was feeding off my fear and enjoying itself. This got so bad for me, that I used to stay awake all night and sleep in the day, because I darn't sleep in the dark. So I put the mirror on e-bay and I said, "I can't be having this" and I put a warning on e-bay, saying that this mirror is extremely haunted. I didn't want to put it into a charity shop where some unsuspecting person would have it. I thought that someone who was into ghosts could buy it at their own risk. Anyway, someone came to pick it up and they said, "Oh we don't care that this mirror is haunted, this is fantastic" and they asked me what exactly was in the mirror, and I told them that someone hung themselves in front of the mirror and that I believed their soul was trapped within the mirror, and that it had caused this awful haunting in my house. And as soon as the mirror went, I expected that the Shadow People and all the crap would go with it, but it didn't! Anyway, two days passed, and the person who took the mirror from me, called me at home and begged me to take the mirror back. They said that they might smash it, and I said "Well good luck". I said that if you break that mirror, and this was my theory, you would release whatever it was into the atmosphere, kind of thing. So he begged me to have it back and I said no. To which he said that he would give it away, and I said "Don't give it to someone unsuspecting, tell the people what's wrong with it. Anyway, many months passed, and my daughter had moved out, but I was still plagued by these 'Shadow People'. There are two parts of the story, I stopped seeing the 'Shadow People' temporarily".

"Some time later, my daughter and I were driving in the car back from my mum's. We had had a bit of a row, so the energy and vibes in the car were a bit low. As we were driving back into my village up Bird's Hill, and that's haunted, I've written about it in one of my books. Well, we had to stop at a low bridge, and we both saw a 'man', well at first we thought it was a man. The best way that I can describe it, was it was like the 'Hat Man' a dark shadow, and he was walking like Michael Jackson when he does the Moon Walk and 'it' was crossing the

162

road, and there was this 4X4 had stopped to let this 'man' (although I don't think it was a man, pass) and halfway across the road, 'it' disappeared. My instincts were, that as soon as I saw this 'man' I had to lock all the doors as I was frightened. At first I thought that it was a normal man but soon realised that it wasn't, that it was something that both my daughter and I had seen at home on various occasions that had plagued us. We couldn't see the reaction of the 4X4 driver, but our reaction was, 'f*****g hell''.

"We are getting poltergeist effects at my home at the moment, not 'Shadow People'. My son moved in last year, he lost his job, he lost his flat it was a difficult time for him, and that started off a poltergeist outbreak. The 'Shadow People' have stopped for now, but occasionally, if I am feeling really low I will sense them drawing in, and I tell them to f**k off, and I light a candle, and I do cleansing with sage, as I have a sage bush outside, and I just literally try not to be frightened, because as soon as you get frightened, that's it. They 'feed' off your fear. They are inter dimensional beings, and another thing as well, because of this 5G and all these energy fields that are around us all the time, I think they use that as a way of getting in. And I think that they are drawn in, in times of terrible crisis. At the moment, due to the Covid, there is a lot of fear, it's almost like food for them"

"One of the things that was happening to me, is that I had a glass vase, I know this isn't the 'Shadow People' but I think that it is all connected. I bought this glass vase, a very heavy vase from an antique shop in Czechoslovakia and I had it on my shelf in the hall and several times it got thrown at me, and I just thought that it had fallen off the shelf or whatever, and the last time I just had a feeling that something horrible was in the hallway near the vase. I walked towards the shelf which held the vase, when all of a sudden it launched itself off the shelf and hit me in the back and nearly knocked me over. So I said to myself that this is going in the bin. And then the energy in the house lifted. When I am doing my psychic work in the kitchen we will have things thrown about in the kitchen. People who I am on the phone to doing their psychic reading will say, "What was that noise"? And I'll say "Oh that was just our kitchen

163

poltergeist". But it mainly happens in the kitchen. I think there is an underground stream or something under our kitchen. Many years ago, we had a homeless chap live with us, and whilst he was living with us, every time he went into the kitchen, he would get knives, cutlery and bowls thrown at him. And I would say to him, "It's your mum", as his mum had passed away. She is telling me that you need to do more in the kitchen and help me. Because I have helped spirits move on and things like that over the years, I have sometimes brought them back with me. Sometimes they try and have a go at me"

"The 'Hat Man', well I can't seem to work him out. He seems to be higher up in the echelons of 'their' society. I wouldn't even say that there is anything human about them, because what kind of entity loves fear? What kind of entity enjoys pain. I feel with this Covid thing, I feel that there are going to be more of these 'Shadow People' around, and the 'Hat Man' seems to be like the boss, possibly, I don't know. In our old house where we lived, an old mill cottage, there were a couple of ghosts in there, and that was very very haunted, but by nice ghosts, so it wasn't a problem. And the kids got used to it, it was just part of living in an old house. Film crews used to come to that house, we had the BBC and also German TV. We had so many film crews that came to that house when I was writing my second book. The world press got involved, because the haunting was really bad. Bowls would move across the room, things would fly up into the air. I said to a chap from the BBC, that if I touch a spoon, it will bend just like Uri Geller did with his spoons. He didn't believe me so I just touched a knife and it just started to bend in front of his eyes"

(MR) "Can you still bend cutlery"?

(NT) "Ah, on occasion I can yes. Teaspoons are best for this. One other thing, there was a chap called Albert Budden who came to my house and took some readings from the house and readings from me, and the story ended up in a newspaper, and it was titled, 'This is the Incredible Electric Woman', because I had all these weird electrical things that were happening to me and in the house. And he said that I have E.M.

164

sensitivity (Electro Magnetic) and that there was a high E.M. reading from my home. And when I held his Geiger counter, it was going really really crazy, and Albert said that it was my energy field that was making it go crazy like this, and that I had a very big energy field around me. I remember as a child watching Uri Geller on T.V. and I got a spoon out of the drawer, and my mum said, "Oh, are you going to do a Uri Geller", I said "Yes". So I stroked the spoon, and the spoon just fell backwards, and mum screamed and ran out of the house. But I couldn't do it after that. I believed in Uri Geller, because it happened to me. Sometimes I just touch things and they just blow up, computers, light switches will just blow. If I'm in a bad mood things will just blow. And Albert Budden said that some people are very sensitive to E.M. fields and probably store up some kind of energy and release it in a burst and that can cause electrical malfunctions. And the amount of electrical appliances, washing machines etc that have blown up near me is unbelievable. Its not so bad now for as I have got older, I feel that my energy field is diminishing, so its not so much of a problem with blowing things up these days. My dad got me started on this, he used to travel around the country for work and he saw so many ghosts. And he used to tell me these stories late at night when I was about eight or nine. We would travel around Scotland every year staying in castles and farm houses, and he would always say that this house is haunted, and it terrified me, (laughs) I was just a kid. And he wasn't frightened of anything. So I think that I have inherited that off him. It's all about energy, psychic energy. I had a row with my son once, it was in the kitchen, and I was on the phone to my friend and I was saying to my son, "Oh for God's sake shut up", and at this point, a knife, a really big knife, like a chef's knife, literally came off the draining board and hit him in the back. He was OK. He works as a psychic as well now, he calls himself Zodiac".

"The poltergeist that we have in my house now, attacks him as well, more so when he is being horrible to me. So the poltergeist sometimes sticks up for me as well (laughs) I'll be down here working and my son is in bed, and I can hear in my bedroom things being thrown around, and whatever energy it

165

is, it is taking out 'its' frustrations. I mean, sometime it's playful and other times its nasty. A few nights ago my son was on the phone doing a reading for a woman, and all of a sudden I heard him yell "MUM," and he ran down the stairs and said that this woman was talking, saying that her husband had left her, when all of a sudden a snarling horrible evil sound came through the phone whilst the woman was talking. But this happens to me quite a lot as well. I'll give someone a reading and there will be another voice on the line. They think that it is someone at my end, but its not. So I think telephones are a conduit for psychic phenomenon to occur. I believe that any kind of electrical or magnetic energy can sometimes create paranormal events. That thunderstorm with the 'Hat Man' allowed him, or gave him the energy to appear, he almost rode the thunderstorm, but my daughter said, there he was. The 'Hat Man' is harmful. I don't think that the 'Shadow People' go back that far, I think that they are more of a modern phenomena. For me, I think that they first came into prominence, in the late 90"s, that's when I started to hear about them. We are in a soup of electrical and magnetic fields, so I think that this enables these inter dimensional 'Shadow People' to come into our world. What is their agenda? That's what we need to ask ourselves. I mean, they made me not being able to sleep at night, I had to change my schedule so I slept in the day and was awake all night working. They ruined my life for some months, it was horrendous".

(MR) "Well Natalie I must thank you for sharing those stories with me. It's been a pleasure speaking with you and I wish you every success in your future ghost Investigations and writings".

(NT) "No problem Malcolm, it was a pleasure speaking with you".

Jez Rackham. *'The 'Hat Man' At The Rehearsal Studio'!*

Our next story comes from a musician, who whilst rehearsing with his band mates during the 1990's, saw something that he will never forget, and he shares that story with us now.

"Church Stowe, and its sister village Upper Stowe, are enviably situated at the behest of a gentle village peak overlooking the rural villages bordering Northants, England, surrounded by undulating hills, open fields, tall aged tree's lining the winding roads of houses unique in heritage style and full of history. Sheepfold Grange stands out, amongst its 2.5 acres, sitting atop a crest of a sweeping long hill, oft used for sledging by the locals in snowy winters, yet equally beautiful relaxing on the gardens veranda on a warm summer afternoon, as the sun catches the hues of the fields lush colours, owned and maintained by the local landowners and farmers. This gorgeous village remains in high demand amongst those hunting houses in desirable, character filled rural retreats. Sheepfold Grange has a number of disused stables, which underwent a development around 1990, and the owners made the decision to convert the stables and barns into a recording and rehearsal studio. My introduction as a musician, afforded me the luxury of being invited many times to play, record, rehearse and produce, a number of projects on the premises, and I got to meet many people, including of course the owners themselves, who warmly allowed the freedom to explore the house and grounds, and to feel wholly welcome and trusted. The house had a history, as it was several hundred years old, and without much surprise, and piqued curiosity, I got to hear of numerous tales of 'experiences' and 'visitations' that defied the natural, and these supernatural encounters fascinated me".

"My own story follows thus, in that it happened at the most unusual of times, it being a hot mid afternoon summers day, and the band I was involved with, were having a busy and timely rehearsal for an approaching show. The day was going well, and as is usual for such situations, time was running away

with itself, and everyone decided to have a late lunch at the main farm house, as we had been practising since 9:00am, having travelled an hour, and it was by now, approaching 2.30pm. At this point, soup and fresh chunky bread was the order of the day, and while everyone headed off to satisfy their appetites, I chose to stay in the studio, to try and locate an issue with a particularly noisy microphone cable that was causing some problems. I made a cup of tea, and was kneeling down between the rehearsal studio door and the equipment P.A. store that led to the outside, when I happened to glance up at the door that led to the outside, as something caught my eye. Beyond the ability to quantify what I was witnessing, I saw a black, densely composed figure, humanoid in shape, grotesquely out of proportion, seemingly formed of what appeared to be dense sooty mist, very 2 dimensional, certainly not of this dimension, absolutely solid, not wraithlike, and I watched it scamper in, deftly jump up onto a P.A. case, then bound from one case or stack to another, almost mischievously, yet chaotically, then appeared to register me just briefly, and jump into the wall and disappear. The creature was approx 3ft tall, very skinny, almost emaciated, had an unusually huge head with a very pronounced and pointed snout, very long hands and very long feet, almost double the size of acceptable proportions. I was entirely incredulous at what I had undeniably witnessed,. and oddly, after about 20 minutes when the rest of the band returned, I felt it was a personal revelation, and that I shouldn't speak of it. The band resumed their positions, and we proceeded to carry on with the practising of our set, when after mere minutes of resuming activity, I noticed one of the singers, Andy, who was placed near the studio door that looked into the P.A. store, visibly stuttering at something he had just seen. We paused, as he was visibly shaken, and I asked if he was OK. He replied that something very strange had happened, and we would be hard pressed to believe him. I said Andy, just tell us exactly what you saw, we are your mates, and to my astonishment, yet somehow secretly knowing, he began to describe the very thing I had also seen. Andy saw it jump out of the wall and run up the glossed yellow stairs into the attic. There was no sensation of dread, or fear, no preceding hyped

168

up moment of expectation, it was simply yet incontestably, two people, in the same place, without prior discussion, witnessing the very same apparition appear, and that led to the conclusion of the authenticity, unquestionably, of what we had genuinely seen. I am still in touch with that guy now, and occasionally it comes up in conversation still, because such visitations witnessed by more than one person, of the same thing, are so rare, yet we experienced it absolutely. There was speculation about hangings there, an oppressive master, and illegal abortions.

Jez Rackham. August 2021

THE SCEPTICAL SLANT

It should be pointed out that there are many people who would disagree with those who say that have seen the fabled 'Hat Man'. There are always two sides to a story, and many sceptics would say that there is no such thing as the 'Hat Man'. It would be remiss of me not to include at least one sceptical view on the 'Hat Man'. And this view comes from a member of the Scottish Society of Psychical Research, Innes Smith, where he talks about gathering 'Hat Man' data, either through the internet or witnesses. He states;

"For what it's worth, I tend to think that such internet born obsessions are just that, internet obsessions. Certainly there is some merit in using sheer numbers to check for patterns in the data, but when you gather together all such 'Hat apparitions' as 'the Hat Man', then it's placing the interpretation before the data. There's much I'm sceptical about in a similar vein, e.g. Black Eyed Children, etc. Trends suggest to me that such experiences are products of cultural expectation bias, rather than evidence of some underlying reality. They don't present compelling evidence for the paranormal, rather the opposite. But, that's my opinion. I'm sure others will disagree. The fact that apparitions vary is fascinating as it is challenging, but can probably all be covered if we believe spiritualists, people see the quality of apparition based on the sender, 'and' the receiver!

For the record, Innes further stated that, and I quote;

"I've been attending lectures at the Scottish Society for Psychical Research since 1993, and joined as a member in 1998 and later joined the Investigation Group in the year 2000. Much has changed since then, most notably the airing of 'Most Haunted' in 2001, when interest in the paranormal and paranormal investigation exploded in popularity. However, with the popular interest and the sensational approach of the media, as well as the dramatic increase in freelance spiritualist mediums and psychics, I spend more of my time combating a Hollywood Horror Movie view of the paranormal, or the bad advice of bad mediums, than investigating the paranormal per se. I do believe that people have anomalous experiences, and there's something definitely going on, but it's important to separate the experience from the belief. In my years of investigating the paranormal, I'd say that what I've learned the most is,

(1) "I use the word 'ambiguous' a lot and",

(2) "People's ability to cope with the paranormal is the same as their ability to cope with any other problem. The problem is a problem because they lack support, people to believe in them, and people to be there for them. Fundamentally whatever the problem with the paranormal is, the solution is social. I'm professionally a freelance writer that mainly works in radio and animation for the BBC".

(Author's Note)

Well it is clear to see from the few examples of the 'Hat Man' and 'Shadow People' sightings above, that people do clearly see this phenomenon. One can also see the clear similarities between a good few of the above accounts. People speak of the fear that they feel whilst viewing these 'entities', and that these 'entities' seem to feed off the fear that they themselves are having whilst watching these disturbing events unfold. Both Lee Dunn and Natalie Osborne Thomason, state quite clearly that they believe that due to the ongoing Covid virus pandemic, the 'Hat Man' and 'Shadow People' sightings are on the increase. Clearly the 'Hat Man' is different from the other entity sightings, for in the main, 'Hat Man' usually tends to stay still and silent in the room, watching intently the victim in the room whilst saying nothing. What purpose does he serve, what is 'he' hoping to achieve? Can 'he' really be feeding off people's fear? Is that what gives him power? Is he some kind of energy vampire? Well I'm afraid we really don't know, all we can do is speculate. That said, all the people that have had the misfortune to see the 'Hat Man', do say that he feeds of their fear. As for the actual 'Shadow People', well these seem different to the 'Hat Man'. They generally are seen to move about as we heard from witness Kathy Cogliano. Does that make them any less fearful? Certainly not. In our next and final chapter, I will take a look at some of the possibilities that might explain the 'Hat Man' and 'Shadow People' phenomenon.

CHAPTER FIVE

The Author's Thoughts

Well we have come to the end of this book, and I dare say that the reader is by now wondering what my own feelings are in regards to Patricia and her daughter Amanda's encounters with not only the 'Hat Man', but the numerous other paranormal encounters that they have had to endure over the years. Well I have devoted my whole life into looking at most aspects of the paranormal, and I'm still trying to fathom it out. I have my own thoughts which I will share with you in a moment. But when I started out on this journey of exploration into the paranormal, I knew that there would be twists and turns, and I knew that it would not all be plain sailing. I knew that I would come across bizarre cases like the one featured in this book. I also knew that many people would not accept these bizarre events, and that perhaps I myself, would get a hard time from the die hard sceptics and those who wouldn't believe in a ghost if they tripped over one. *(well, believe it or not, people do witness solid looking ghosts!)* This subject that we call the paranormal, is indeed very bizarre. It's strange, it makes you wonder about reality and what is real and what is not. Nobody in this field is an expert, including me. All I can do as a researcher, is to listen to the people who tell me these accounts and not to judge, but to weigh up the testimony and see if it rings true. True in the sense that after all my research, that what is left behind is a real and bona fide paranormal event, for one always has to be careful about being deceived, about being duped into believing a particular story. Some may see Patricia and Amanda's story as being totally unbelievable, well that's their prerogative. Who said life would be easy? Who said things are just black and white? Who knows all the answers? People need to realise that we do indeed live in strange times, not everything is so cut and dried. Mankind is learning all the time. We shouldn't turn our back on things like this, simply because it appears outlandish and improper. We will never learn anything if we just turn and hide from things of this nature. Some scientists may see the paranormal as a subject to steer well clear of, and who can blame them? The paranormal is bizarre, it is crazy, sometimes its hard for even me to get my head around it, but at least I know never to turn my back on it. I am here to get answers, and, I must point out, unmask any fakers who are out to pull the wool over not only my eyes, but 'yours' as well.

All paranormal researchers are looking for answers, some researchers sadly have their mind already made up, and will come away with bizarre explanations for these subjects which are no nearer to the truth than they can comprehend. In this our final chapter, I aim to go through as many possibilities that I can, to shed some light on the experiences of Patricia and Amanda. There may be some possibilities that I might have missed, but I'd like to think that I've covered the main ones. Does the answer to what Patricia and Amanda have experienced lie within the possibilities to follow? Or am I way off the mark? Like all the books that I've written, I try to be objective and provide alternative explanations, just like I did with my book, *'The Dechmont Woods UFO Incident'*, that book had eleven possible theories that could/might explain that astounding event. This book is no different. So with no disrespect to Patricia and Amanda, (and I'm sure they would be the first to agree with me that I 'should' look to explain and understand what could be alternative answers to account for what they have experienced), let us look at some of those possibilities, for not to do so, would not be in keeping with the nature of paranormal research. Sceptics will always ask, did I think of this, did I think of that. Well I want to make it clear, I am no doctor, neither am I a scientist, all I am, is a human being with an inquisitive mind, eager to get to the answer of life's mysteries. The following information I have gathered together from various health web sites on the internet. So, again with no disrespect to Patricia and Amanda, let us now take a look at what 'might' cause the visions that both Patricia and Amanda encountered.

SLEEP PARALYSIS.

There is a condition called 'sleep paralysis,' which does have some similar parameters of which both Patricia and Amanda experienced during their encounters, as you will see below. The main symptoms of sleep paralysis are.

- A feeling of being unable to move or speak while falling asleep or while waking up.
- Being conscious of ones surroundings.
- Feeling like 'something', or 'someone' is in the room with you when you know there isn't.
- An intense fear, that initially you can't put your finger on.
- A feeling of pressure on your body, legs, chest, or head.

BUT WHAT CAUSES SLEEP PARALYSIS?

Sleep paralysis is commonly felt to occur during the transition between wakefulness and sleep (Hypnagogic) or when you are waking up (Hypnopompic) It's been stated that this 'state' occurs in at least 20% of the populace. The most frightening thing about this state, is the fact, that in most accounts, you are awake, but your whole body is shut down, its paralysed. This effect is called 'muscle atonia'. This 'state' may last from anything from a few minutes, to several minutes. In this 'state', only your eyes can move. On record we have people who have desperately tried to call out for help, but nine times out of ten, you can only raise a whisper at best. Probably the most unnerving thing about being under sleep paralysis, is the sense of suffocating. You are short of breath, and every breath feels like a mission. Whilst this is going on, some people may see what they believe to be a Demon, or an old lady, (known as the old hag syndrome) sitting on your chest. They may look down at you, mock you, scowl at you, and call you names. Some people state that they are fully awake whilst

174

all this is going on, whilst others claim only to be partially awake. Some people also claim to leave their body at this point, and go into what's known as an 'astral projection,' where they can visit friends and family both near and far. Or, in some cases, they may just float and hover above their bed looking down at themselves, which, in anyone's book, is also very frightening an unnerving.

THEN WE HAVE CONDITIONS RELATED TO SLEEP PARALYSIS.

<u>NARCOLEPSY</u> (Also known as: Gelineau Syndrome)
The main symptoms of Narcolepsy are.

* Excessive daytime sleepiness. Sudden attacks of sleep, even during activities.
* Feeling if you have little alertness for the rest of the day.
* Finding it hard to focus and complete work tasks.
* You may have a sudden loss of muscle tone called cataplexy.
* Sleep paralysis. (As stated above)
* Hallucinations. Imagining things in the room that truly do not exist.

<u>NIGHT TERRORS</u>

The main symptoms of night terrors are.

* Screaming out loudly. Crying, or talking gibberish.
* Sitting up in bed and looking around wildly for no reason.
* Thrash about and kick at the covers for no apparent reason.
* Show aggressive behaviour if someone tries to restrain you.
* Wide open and staring eyes.
* Sweating profusely.

175

- Breathing heavily.
- Racing pulse.
- Dilated pupils.

EXPLODING HEAD SYNDROME.

The main symptoms of Exploding Head Syndrome are.

* Hearing loud noises when falling asleep or waking up.
* The noise can be frightening and cause alarm.
* You may see a strong flash of light.
* There is no pain associated with this effect.
* *(You will be pleased to note, that your head doesn't physically explode with this condition).*

PARASOMNIA.

The main symptoms of Parasomnia are.

- Involuntary sleep disorders, such as, moving, speaking, or walking around during sleep.
- Waking up from sleep in a state of confusion and disorientation.
- You may also find that you have an inability to move or speak when waking up or drifting off to sleep.
- Finding bruises, cuts, or other wounds that you were sure, were not there before.
- Excessive daytime fatigue.

HALLUCINATIONS

OK, first of all we have to realise that there are many components and aspects to a hallucination. We can break them down to a combination of events and effects such as, 'visual hallucinations', 'auditory hallucinations', 'tactile hallucinations', and 'olfactory hallucinations'. Of course hallucinations may be the result of taking drugs, indeed a lot of them are. But some are pure medical conditions. Let us a take a look at what each one comprises of.

VISUAL HALLUCINATIONS

Visual hallucinations are something that the individual will experience whether on drugs or having a medical episode. They will perceive an experience of something that is not there. Effectively, it's something like you are having a dream, but in point of fact you are fully awake. Most of the time, these type of hallucinations are associated with sleep paralysis which I have mentioned above. They can appear very clear and concise, and hard to define where reality starts, and reality ends. These hallucinations can be of many things, from weird shapes, weird colours, horrible visions of men, women, children and a whole lot more. More often, these visions/hallucinations, comprise of seeing a dark figure, a shadow, or even what one might construe as a ghost! Some people have seen numerous people in a room with them, either directly, or just outside their peripheral vision. Visual hallucinations can also comprise of a shimmering in the room, or seeing just parts of a human body, animals, or even bugs!

AUDITORY HALLUCINATIONS

Primarily, these are more sounds than visions, but can equally prove distressing. People may hear talking in the room, sometimes even in a foreign language! The individual may also hear people laughing, or screaming, or even whispering. Auditory hallucinations can also comprise of a loud and annoying buzzing or static sound. Also on record, are the sounds of footsteps in the room when no one is there. There can be knocking on the furniture and a whole range of other auditory sounds.

TACTILE HALLUCINATIONS

This form of hallucination, leans more towards sensing and feeling. In other words, some people claim that they are being touched, or interfered with! Some people can also experience a pressure being exerted onto their chest or other parts of their body. Moreover, it is the distressing feeling of something 'holding them down' or in other words, 'pressing them down in the bed', our thoughts may go to Sharon Cooper mentioned earlier in this book, who had this exact same feeling of being pushed down into her bed as did Patricia and Amanda. Other aspects of a tactile hallucination, is a tingling feeling, or even numbness, or that one's body is vibrating. Other people have reported a sense of either floating, flying, or falling. Probably the most distressing aspect of a tactile hallucination, is not just the pressure exerted on one's chest or body, but the sense that you are physically being dragged from your bed! Even worse, is the physical sensation of being raped!, which, as we have read earlier, occurred to Sharon Cooper. Some people feel cold with a tactile hallucination and experience the feeling of bugs or critters crawling all over their body, which in anyone's book, must be most distressing. There is also a feeling as if someone is standing next to you breathing in your ear!

OLFACTORY HALLUCINATIONS

This particular hallucination has elements that don't always feature in the main stay of a main hallucination, that said, it can still be part of it. This hallucination is more down to smells. Smelling anything from cigar smoke to perfumes that the person knows should not be in the room with them. Make no bones about it, these type of hallucinations mentioned above, can, for those people who have experienced them, be pretty terrifying. They may feel that they are about to die, or that something bad is going to happen to them. Some may think that they are having a stroke. Some people state how real everything seems when it is occurring.

SUMMING UP THE HALLUCINATION THEORY

In summing up the hallucination aspect of trying to provide a potential answer to account for what Patricia and Amanda have gone through. I can only say that, yes, there does appear to be elements of the above possibilities, that both Patricia and Amanda have experienced, and you don't need to be a brain surgeon to expect that the sceptics will say, *"Well there lies your answer Mr Robinson, its all down to hallucinations"* That's as may be. But let's be honest here, whilst some of the above may match the symptoms that both Patricia and Amanda had (and are still having) that is not the be all and end all of the answer. Patricia and Amanda experienced things mostly in a waking state, and not at night. These were daily occurrences, viewed on a few occasions, by other people. Therefore, if we still go along with the hallucination aspect, then those other people must have hallucinated with the Hessions as well! For me, the author of this book, I would say that perhaps some, but certainly not all, of Patricia and Amanda's night time paranormal events, may, and I stress 'may', have been down to hallucinations or sleep paralysis, but I'm not sure, and I could be very wrong on that.

So if we are not talking about sleep paralysis or hallucinations being the result and answer to what both Patricia and Amanda have been going through, then what else is there to question? Well, there are a few things that I feel I should bring into play here, because if I don't, the sceptics sure would!

OTHER POSSIBILITIES!

A HOAX

Sadly in life, many people try to gain a better life for themselves by doing a whole lot of things that may not always be in their own and other people's best interests! And not all of these shady deals bear fruit. Some, having tried ever so hard in their life to better themselves, may resort to trying to gain and enhance their life by deceit, and there are numerous ways on how this can come about. For instance, someone may be desperate to get out of their house and they have tried everything to do so, but nothing has worked, maybe their last resort would be to fake a ghost story, present it to their local council, and hope that they may get re-housed! That may not be as far fetched as you think, it has been tried by others. Do I think that this was the case here with the Hession family? No I do not. I honestly don't think that the Hession family would go to all these lengths to do something like this. Believe it or not, they are happy in their house, yes they could do without the bizarre occurrences, but it is their family home.

MONETARY GAIN

So what about monetary gain? What I mean by this is, let's go with the scenario of a family making up a ghost story to get a better house, they might sell their story to a National newspaper or magazine? Not only could they be re-housed, but they would also have some money in their back pocket to enjoy as well! Well, that's not as far fetched as it sounds. Human beings (or some of them) will go to extraordinary lengths to gain that extra few dollars/pounds to line their pockets, it's human nature, not a great side to human nature I'll admit, but human nature nonetheless. Let me tell you this dear reader, the Hession family have not asked for a single penny for their story to be told in this book. They are just happy for their bizarre events to be told. If anything, things might get even worse when this book gets published, as perhaps so called friends and family may turn on them. They may get pointed out in the street by strangers who may be aware of this book and who the Hessions are, and poke fun at them. These type of stories do little to help the poor victims of psychic attack, if anything, they may make them worse. So a lot of credit must go to Patricia and Amanda for coming forward. And let's be honest here, we can't even say that they are creating a false story just to gain popularity, for as paranormal history has shown us, quite the reverse can often happen. People have been chased out of town or had their windows broken by people who just 'don't understand'. I'm not throwing the baby out with the bathwater here, I appreciate that there are people out there in the big wide world who do have medical episodes, who do have visions etc. That opens up another question, because if people have these experiences that Patricia and Amanda have gone through, but are just suffering a medical episode, or indeed are on drugs, why are they experiencing the same type of visions as Patricia and Amanda? How can that be? Would hallucinations not comprise of something else? Who knows, that question is best asked by a better person than me. As stated, I am not a doctor, I don't have any medical qualifications or abilities. I know how to put a plaster on and that's about it! As stated above, the medical information that I have given earlier, I had to source from medical web sites. I then cross referenced them to ensure that I was not missing anything and quoting the conditions incorrectly.

ARE YOU MAKING THIS UP?

I decided to ask Patricia and Amanda right off the bat, questions that the sceptics of this book would surely have asked. I just hoped that both Patricia and Amanda would not take offence and would still be willing to speak to me. And although admittedly both Patricia and Amanda had already told me that they were not making these stories up, I still had to ask. Here are those direct questions I asked them and the relevant answers.

(Malcolm) *"Patricia, are you making this story up to get a better house"?*

(Patricia and Amanda) *"Most certainly not, as my mother left our home for us in our will. And, just for the record, I have always told you and others, that both myself and Amanda, along with others, are giving you our life story solely to you as a gift from us. We do not want any payment or royalties, as this book is 'yours' Amanda and I only want our truth to be told in order to be of help to others who may be experiencing similar events. I want them to understand that unfortunately what they are going through is real, and that they are not alone, as our story is just one of many out there, and that there are plenty of individuals sites and groups willing to offer their services".*

(Malcolm) *"Have you ever tried to sell your story to a National newspaper or magazine to earn a few euros"?*

(Patricia and Amanda) *"No, never in my life. You Malcolm are the only person I trust, and our story is yours alone, gifted to you, as you were one of the first to believe in us".*

(Malcolm) *"Did your birth parents (or adopted parents) ever witness what you and Amanda saw, in regards to the 'Hat Man' and other strange events"?*

(Patricia and Amanda) *"Barbara my biological mother, had indeed seen things but wished to forget them, as it did her mother no good, because Barbara's mother was a 'wise woman' a Hedge Witch (ie, she dealt with nature things, white magic etc) as many of the women and some men in her family did. She saw things that were unexplainable, because she was descended from Irish and Amazique gypsy tribes. She believed that her mother was diagnosed with psychosis and institutionalised for seeing things. Both my adopted mother Norah, and my father John, had missing time on two occasions, and I am not sure about my father, but my mother and I saw bright red lights appear in every window of our Motel room that we once stayed in. I believe my father John, saw the 'Hat Man' in the cellar of our property at Watts Street Malden Massachusetts, as he had lots of bright florescent lights installed several months after I saw him. Both Amanda and I believe that our adopted mother Norah, started to see things a few years before her death, due to the fact that she always slept in the dark with the curtains closed, but later she slept with them wide open with the moonlight and my neighbours solar lights beaming in. She was very religious, and would not talk about these things when in St Luke's hospital Renalagh Dublin following radiation treatment for her brain tumour. She also saw a large blue figure crowned with flowers, and the telly turning on by itself and flicking through stations at the time of her death. My birth father, John C. Hession, passed away after a heart attack in 1980",*

(Malcolm) *"Have you or Amanda ever taken drugs other than prescription drugs, which might have made you see what you have seen"?*

182

(Patricia and Amanda) *"No we have not, and we are both happy to get tested on such, on any date and time of your choosing. We only drink on occasion".*

And whilst the sceptics may say that both Patricia and Amanda were lying in answering the above questions, the fact of the matter is, that we are dealing here with two family members who would rather not have these troubling events transpire in their home. Bringing to the world's attention about these horrible events, may make things worse! And by that I mean, they make get visited from people who have read this book and want to see this haunted house. Not only that, they may have to endure phone calls from the media all looking for that sensational story. So by coming forward, they are not doing themselves any favours, other than sharing these events in the hope that those who are also going through these terrible events, may get in touch with someone who can offer some help.

BUT WHAT IS THE 'HAT MAN'?

We've heard a lot about the 'Hat Man' in this book, but what is 'he' (if he even is a he!) The main crux of Patricia and Amanda's encounters, has of course been the 'Hat Man'. This is the creature, Demon, call him what you will, that has invaded the Hession's lives, and caused them untold misery. The 'Hat Man' is not a new thing, 'he' has been around for many hundreds of years, and been seen by many thousands of people world wide. Is 'he' an illusion? Are people suffering from some form of 'global psychosis'? The 'Hat Man' sometimes referred to as the 'Grey Man' or the 'Shadow Man', is an entity that is usually described as a man wearing a wide brimmed hat and wearing a long trench coat. In some encounters, the 'Hat Man' is described as wearing a cowboy hat, or a fedora trilby like hat, or an older top hat. There is a more defined difference between the 'Hat Man' and 'Shadow People'. The 'Hat Man' usually has dark facial features, and sometimes people claim to see red staring eyes. The 'Hat Man' appears quite tall in height, although other sightings of 'him', have him appearing as quite small. The down side of seeing the 'Hat Man' (not that there is a good side) is that he always brings with him, a sense of foreboding, of fear. There are some researchers who believe that he feeds of the individual's fear. He seems to latch onto people's pain and suffering. He may often speak to the terrified individual giving them threats and warnings, these may come in the form of bizarre and unsolvable riddles. What also sets the 'Hat Man' apart form 'Shadow People', is the fact that the 'Hat Man' moves like a human, walks and behaves like a human. So, what does that make him? A spirit, a Demon, or something else? To some people, the 'Hat Man' sometimes is not a 'one off' event, and may appear several times to the distressed witness throughout their lives.

Sceptics might rightly ask,

"But surely this in part, could be put down to some people's fear of the dark, and are just imagining this 'Hat Man' figure"

Well, again, to a degree, this could be true. As a child I was often frightened of the dark, and imagined all sorts of monsters lurking under the bed or behind the curtains, and some nights I couldn't get to sleep because of my over active imagination, and some children might misconstrue dark shapes in the bedroom as something else. I'm not saying that was the case with the Hession family, far from it, there is way more to what they experienced than dark shapes in the bedroom. Researcher and writer Heidi Hollis, the author of *'The 'Hat Man': The True Story of Evil Encounters'*, is of the opinion that the 'Hat Man' is a demonic entity, or a minion of the Devil. This belief is shared by quite a number of researchers. Both Patricia and Amanda state that they have never seen the 'Hat Man's feet, or if he is wearing shoes. Patricia firmly believes that the 'Hat Man' is Lucifer. The 'Hat Man' was but one element of what the Hession family had to endure.

So, dear reader, what was the outcome of this troublesome case? Well I'm afraid to say that things are still happening. I asked a number of Irish paranormal groups to get involved, some did, some didn't. For those that did, the events remained. Patricia has had her house blessed on numerous occasions by her own Catholic Priests, and still the paranormal events occur. She has had other religious and non religious people coming to her home, all offering help in one way or another, but still the events transpired. Patricia was given a very powerful prayer many years ago by an exorcist in America, Father Peter Rooky, but again, this hasn't had much affect. She was also given another powerful prayer by a friend on Facebook to try, which she is still trying. I can only hope, that by bringing this book out regarding what Patricia and her daughter have had to endure, it will not only show you the reader, but those of an enquiring mind, that we are indeed living in strange times.

WHAT THE HESSIONS BELIEVE IS GOING ON.

With all that has been going on with Patricia and Amanda, I decided to ask her for her own opinions as to what had been going on throughout her life. Did she herself, have any ideas, and if so, could she share them with me? Well share them with me she did, and the following is quite an intriguing collection of disturbing stories. First she spoke about what the small grey beings that both herself and Amanda had witnessed. She said.

"There are both positive and negative Greys, just like we have both positive and negative in humanity. Unfortunately if a human being arrived unannounced in your home, day or night and abducted you or your loved ones, and performed various tests and surgical procedures, in an aggressive manner, without your consent since childhood, what would you do? My daughter and I have been terrorised since our childhood by various beings, mostly the Greys, to the point of dreaded fear, constantly being ill from one extent to the other. Some of our symptoms are unexplainable".
"Amanda and I both have 'others' whom I call my brothers and sisters of Christ, my Sky Family that we do not fear, but let me say this once. Anyone who thinks I am a crack pot, please proceed to invite me at your own request, to have a polygraph

performed on me in relation to all the above, and what I have experienced during my life. Amanda and I are still trying to fit all the pieces together. If you believe in God, any God, then remember that Lucifer wanted to be like God. The Greys also create life forms taken from us, through sperm and ova. They all want power and control in more ways than one! None of them communicated with me or my daughter over a cup of tea, so to speak, they just came and paralysed us, then took from us what they wanted, to the point I felt I was going insane. Thankfully Tim Richards, the hypnotherapist we saw a few years ago, made some sense of it all for us. If they are changing and cloning our D.N.A. for evolution, for humanity, or for a better world, etc. Why all the secrecy on their part? All they have to do is ask us to participate. I believe they are working alongside dark forces for their own advancement. We are of God, we have souls that live on after our body/vessel dies. THEY HAVE NO SOUL and will therefore never return to their Heavenly abode. And no matter how they try over time, they will never be successful in creating replicas of us, as we are created in the image and likeness of God Himself, our essence, our energy, our very soul belongs to HIM. Not them!"

BUT WHY?

At this point in my communications with Pat, I asked her 'why' she felt that these things were continuing to happen to both her and Amanda, she replied.

"I now believe this, as crazy as it sounds Malcolm, that we are protected by a higher realm, yet evil does persist. Amanda and I were Blessed with the Holy Chrism by a Priest, Father Tony, in our Parish of St. Benedict's, here in Kilbarrack, Dublin due to these beings holding power over us, especially me at times. My mother, now deceased, said I used to make strange gestures with my hands and fingers as a child, and I would chatter to myself as if in conversation. When my daughter Amanda was a child, she did exactly the very same! We are the same in many ways! Sometimes we say we are like cloned twins. Both Amanda and I have seen too many various

186

types of beings, crafts, lights, shadows, and anomalies, whilst many others may only have seen a few in their lifetime".

"My next door neighbour Mr. Paul Sullivan and his wife, were witness in my home, to some of the bizarre happenings. They were terrified, and told Paul's brother who is a Priest, Father Dan Sullivan, also a Chaplain in Beaumont Hospital here in Dublin. My own uncle, now deceased, was a Franciscan living in La Verna retreat centre in South Africa, he used to be an Exorcist, and said that my daughter and I needed Deliverance, but Father Tony only prayed and Blessed us with Holy Chrism. We slept well for approximately two weeks, but unfortunately they came back. They always come and go. I believe from past experience that the Greys work under Shadow Beings. The 'Hat Man', then Demonic beings etc. Each has a role, like a community of ants, bees, and animals. We all have our job to do in accordance to a higher power, but I am still trying to piece it all together, and may never know the full truth in this life".

(Author's Note) I then asked how far, and to what lengths Patricia and Amanda had gone to try and get some peace from what had been happening to them. She replied.

"As I've said before, we've had Holy water, statues, and relics all blessed in our house, all to no avail. We've even spread salt around the house, again to no avail, as they still come. In my Roman Catholic faith, it is stated that Evil will not, and cannot enter, where there is Holy water etc. Well these are beyond evil, and can possess our house in other ways. I believe the Greys are linked to Demons, as they both are of a superior intelligence to us, and have the ability to change and manipulate matter. One must again think outside the box and ask, 'what is it they want from us'? What do we have that is so valuable to them? Why have they not destroyed us? our planet? I believe it is our very soul that lives on for all eternity that they are after. For starters, they want to be Gods, to create, but Almighty God created us, therefore our soul, our very essence is his, and to him we shall return. They cannot! They will not be able through time, to create a living soul. Our body is only a

187

vessel, it is the light of the divine they want. Anyway, that is my feeling. We are living as if in a game of the Sims. Not everything is as seems to be! I would not say I am brave, just fed up. Tired of not knowing how to help others like my daughter and I to put an end to these abductions and tests. I need answers, some have good experiences with some Greys, we have not".

(Author's Note)   I also asked Patricia's feelings about history, and what she felt about her experiences as being similar to other world wide accounts. She replied.

"Special knowledge can also come from the darker realms of the occult, or one can achieve this from their faith, such as I. Various beings are of higher intelligence then us, and many have come to Earth in the past to teach us, as in the Native Americans, Egypt, Machu Picchu, and the Nazca lines. Many various tribes and nations around the globe have had encounters with other worldly beings for the good of mankind, yet the Greys abduct and take us against our will, for their own secret agenda in collaboration with our governments all in secret. Remember knowledge is power and many out there thirst for it"!

FINAL WORDS

I asked Patricia what final words would she give to the sceptics who, after reading this book, might be saying about her own and daughter's experiences, she replied.

"Amanda and I know there are sceptics and others who like to have a go at people like us, who say that it's all a load of codswallop. They are entitled to their opinion. But until you have walked in our shoes and experienced the terrifying things that we have, then you would know for sure, that these things are real, very real. We only hope that whoever reads your book Malcolm, will understand that these things are happening, not just to us, but to others as well, maybe even the people reading

your book. And if anything we say sparks something in them to be brave enough to come forward and to seek help, then we will have done something positive. I just want our experiences to help others who may be enduring the same paranormal occurrences that have been happening to us, and for them to know that they are 'not crazy' and they are not alone. I am honoured to have you as a true friend. Thank you once again for believing in us and listening and caring, and helping. For not just my daughter and I, but for the countless others who just need someone on their side. Who will be 'their' voice and make some sense of it all? Although after all these years since my childhood in dealing with both positive and negative beings, I have come to the conclusion that maybe, just maybe, we are meant to have them in our lives for our own personal growth and development. Or from my own understanding and feeling, they could be from my Ancestry, past lives and attached to our DNA".

THE END
(Or is it!)

Just as I was preparing to send the book to the publishers, I received an e-mail from Patricia Hession (28th August 2021) saying that she had another strange experience the previous night. Here is what she said.

"Last night about 03:45am, I woke up from my sleep as I felt my duvet being pulled over my face. I reached out my hand to push it down, and touched an all too familiar hand trying to pull it back up. I grabbed onto its hand and held firmly while reaching for my phone under my pillow in order to take a photo, but my phone wasn't there? I said I'm not going to hurt you, you can trust me, please, I just want to talk with you to understand you better. Let me see you. I pulled down the duvet to see a tall, thin faced Grey staring down at me, but then it seemed to transform into a human looking man right before my eyes. I said, I know. I've said many times that you and the reptilians are evil, along with the 'Hat Man', but it's because of

189

the paralysing fear and terror you install in us, as well as coming here in the middle of the night with all your secrecy about what you are doing to us. He said telepathically, you are not paralysed now. I said "Who are you"?, "Are we a part of you"? He said "yes" and "no"! No further explanation. I asked him, what are you doing to us? and he said "Altering your DNA structure for time on earth, as we have no time". "We have done so much that your human mind cannot comprehend or allow you to". It then looked emotional, a look I've never seen in them as it spoke telepathically, again saying "We are not destructive, we did not cause you any harm". I said "Yes you do"! "You all do! Mental torture, blockages, paralysis and fear". He said, "We have known you through many lifetimes, both as spirit and human. We are here to make the necessary changes needed, as humans are destructive". Then he showed me images in my mind of war, poverty, greed, pollution, and world disasters, and the effects we are causing to our planet and it's creatures! He again said we are not destructive and vanished"!

"I sat up on the edge of my bed, and Amanda woke up asking me if I was OK? It was nearly half four in the morning. I told Amanda what happened. She said she never heard anything, but felt uneasy in her sleep. I looked for my phone thinking it fell under my bed, but found it this morning on my window sill! I'm not sure if there were one 'being' or two. But I wasn't scared last night. I believe now that the book is finished, it wants others to know what it told me. I honestly don't remember anything else, but I did ask him where they're from and other questions, but can't remember the answers as it might have blocked them out of my mind, and only wants me to remember what it wants me to write about. I feel this is important for the book, as its 'his' message he is giving me to others.

Now it is the end
(or is it just the beginning!)

REFERENCES

Terrifying 'Hat Man' Witnessed by Thousands of People. Slapped Ham Web Site.

'What Are the Common Scary Symptoms of Sleep Paralysis'? (verywellhealth.com)

Wikipedia.

FURTHER READING

Borley Postcript. Peter Underwood. White House Publications, P.O. Box 65, Haslemere, GU27 1XT, England. ISBN 0-9537721-1-X

Encyclopedia of Ghosts and Spirits. John and Anne Spencer. Headline Book Publishing of 338 Euston Road, London, England, NW1 3BH. ISBN 0 7472 7169 0.

Ghosts Taverns of the North East. Darren W. Ritson and Michael J Hallowell. Amberley Publishing, The Hill, Stroud, Gloucestershire, England, GL5 4EP. ISBN978-1-4456-0753-5.

Haunted Gardens. Peter Underwood. Amberley Publishing, Cirencester Road Chalford, Stroud, Gloucestershire, GL6 8PE. ISBN 978-184868-261-0

Haunted Wales. Peter Underwood. Amberley Publishing, Cirencester Road Chalford, Stroud, Gloucestershire, GL6 8PE. ISBN 978-184868-2634

Haunted Pubs And Inns of Derbyshire. Jill Armitage. Amberley Publishing, Amberley Publishing, Cirencester Road Chalford, Stroud, Gloucestershire, GL6 8PE. ISBN 978-1-4456-0464-0

More Angelsey Ghosts. Bunty Austin. Amberley Publishing, The Hill, Stroud, England, UK. ISBN 978-1-4456-0332-2

Paranormal Bath. Michael Cady. Amberley Publishing, Cirencester Road Chalford, Stroud, Gloucestershire, GL6 8PE. ISBN 1848681763

Paranormal Dorset. Roger Gutteridge. Amberley Publishing, Cirencester Road Chalford, Stroud, Gloucestershire, GL6 8PE. ISBN 978-1-84868-394-5.

Paranormal Hertfordshire. Damien O Dell. Amberley Publishing, Cirencester Road Chalford, Stroud, Gloucestershire, GL6 8PE. ISBN 978-1-84868-118-7

Paranormal Leicester. Stephen Butt. Amberley Publishing, Cirencester Road Chalford, Stroud, Gloucestershire, GL6 8PE. ISBN 978-1-84868-462-1

Paranormal Lancashire. Daniel Codd. Amberley Publishing, Cirencester Road Chalford, Stroud, Gloucestershire, GL6 8PE. ISBN 978-4456-0658-3

Paranormal North East. Darren W. Ritson. Amberley Publishing, Cirencester Road Chalford, Stroud, Gloucestershire, GL6 8PE. ISBN 978-1-84868-196-5

Paranormal South Tyneside. Michael J Hallowell. Amberley Publishing, Cirencester Road Chalford, Stroud, Gloucestershire, GL6 8PE. ISBN 978-1-84868-730-1

Paranormal Surrey. Marq English. Amberley Publishing, Cirencester Road Chalford, Stroud, Gloucestershire, GL6 8PE. ISBN 978-1-84868-896-4

Paranormal Sussex. David Scanlan. Amberley Publishing, Cirencester Road Chalford, Stroud, Gloucestershire, GL6 8PE. ISBN 978-1-84868-462-1

Paranormal Case Files of Great Britain (Volume 1) Malcolm Robinson. Publish Nation. www.publishnation.co.uk 2010 & 2017. ISBN: 978-1907126-06-2

Paranormal Case Files of Great Britain (Volume 2) Malcolm Robinson. Publish Nation. www.publishnation.co.uk 2016. ISBN: 9781-3268-74-22-3

Paranormal Case Files of Great Britain (Volume 3) Malcolm Robinson. Publish Nation. www.publishnation.co.uk 2018. ISBN: 978-0244-11172-4

Psychic Quest. Natalie Osbourne Thomason. Claireview Books, Hillside House, The Square, Forest Row, East Sussex, RH18 5ES. ISBN 1-902-636-34-1

More Things You Can Do When You're Dead. Tricia J. Robertson. (2015) White Crow Books. www.whitecrowbooks.com ISBN. 978-1910121-44-3

Seeing Ghosts. Hilary Evans. John Murray 50 Albemarle Street London England W1S 4BD. ISBN 0-7195-5492-6.

Scottish Haunts and Poltergeists II. JSPR Vol. 42, March 1964, pp.223-7. Lambert, G W.

Supernatural North. Darren W. Ritson. Amberley Publishing November. 2013. ISBN: 9781848682771

This House Is Haunted. The True Story of a Poltergeist (1980) Guy Lyon Playfair. White Crow Books. ISBN: 978-1907661785

The Encyclopedia of Ghosts and Spirits. (Volume 2) John and Anne Spencer. 2001 Headline Publishing. ISBN: 0-7472-7169-0

The South Shields Poltergeist. Darren W. Ritson & Michael J. Hallowell. The History Press, October 2009. ISBN. 0752452746

The Ghost Handbook. John and Anne Spencer. (1998) MacMillan Publishers Ltd. ISBN: 0-7522-1165-X

The Hat Man. The True Story of Evil Encounters: Heidi Hollis. Amazon.co.uk 9780983040194

Things You Can Do When You're Dead. Tricia J. Robertson. White Crow Books (2013) www.whitecrowbooks.com ISBN. 978-1908733-60-3

Yorkshire Stories of the Supernatural. Andy Owen.
Countryside Books, 3 Catherine Road, Newbury Berkshire, England, U.K. ISBN 1-85306-594-3

U.K. PARANORMAL SOCIETIES:

ASSAP. (The Association for the Study of Anomalous Phenomena) assap@assap.org 020 8798 3981 http://www.assap.ac.uk/index.html

SSPR. (The Scottish Society for Psychical Research). 020 7937 8984 https://www.spr.ac.uk/link/scottish-society-psychical-research

SEMR. (Scottish Earth Mysteries Research) Ron Halliday. https://www.facebook.com/ron.halliday.18

SPI Scotland. (Strange Phenomena Investigations) Alyson Dunlop https://spiscotland.wordpress.com/ spiscotland@gmail.com

SPI Anglia Region. (Strange Phenomena Investigations) David Young. https://www.facebook.com/groups/358025484712267/

Scottish Paranormal. Scottish Paranormal | Facebook

The Ghost Club. https://ghostclub.org.uk

TO CONTACT THE AUTHOR

Research group Strange Phenomena Investigations (SPI) are always interested to hear from anyone who believe that they may have had a UFO or paranormal experience, or indeed may have a photograph or piece of film footage which may appear to show something paranormal. If so, please contact the author at the address below.
(All submissions will be treated in confidence)

Malcolm Robinson,
74 Craigview,
Sauchie,
Clackmannanshire,
Scotland,
FK10 3HF

You can e-mail the author direct at malckyspi@yahoo.com
Facebook: www.facebook.com/malcolm.robinson2

"More scientific discoveries have been made in the last 100 years than in the whole history of mankind put together. Something that seems outrageous to one generation, becomes perfectly normal to the following generation. All the thoughts and conclusions of our ancestors, are only of academic interest to us now"

Professor Archie Roy. FRSE, FRAS was Professor Emeritus of Astronomy in the University of Glasgow.
Born 24th June 1924 - Died 27th December 2012.

Printed in Great Britain
by Amazon

80068257R00119